THE **RIGHT STOCK**
AT THE **RIGHT TIME**

THE RIGHT STOCK
AT THE RIGHT TIME

Prospering in the Coming Good Years

LARRY WILLIAMS

WILEY

JOHN WILEY & SONS, INC.

ACKNOWLEDGMENTS

This book would never been possible without books and research that went before. I want to specifically thank Yale Hirsch, of the *Stock Traders Almanac*, and Steve Moore and Nick Colley of Moore Research.

The high-yield strategy could not have been accomplished without the efforts of Bill Aronin, Joe Getts, and Lisa Liang at Qualitative Analytics. Without my able assistant, Jennifer Wells, this book, and all my other work, would never get done. Nor would this book have seen the light of day without the support and attention of Pamela Van Geissen. Tom DeMark was a great sounding board for many of the ideas and my best cheerleader. Finally, a personal note of thanks to Harvey Levine, who kept me running in more ways than he knows, and Louis Stapelton for the title idea.

We are all indebted for the assistance these wonderful people, especially Carla, provided in helping me present my vision of what will happen in the next few years.

And finally I would like to point out what my best five investments have been: my children, Kelley, Jason, Sara, Michelle, and Paige. Thanks, gang, for many years of the best returns of my life.

CONTENTS

CONTENTS

PREFACE

This story begins in 1962, the year I first began studying stock market prices. I had no knowledge of why the stock market crashed that year, other than what was released in the newspapers: President Kennedy had attacked the steel industry, prohibiting any increase in steel prices. That bit of bad business news knocked the stock market down hundreds of points. The newspapers, then as now, were filled with horror stories of people losing money, and of how bad the economy was. Many cried that this was the beginning of another 1929-like era.

In hindsight, however, it was not a time to sell stocks; it was a time to buy stocks. October 1962 began a huge up move that would not culminate in a top until February 1966 when the Dow Jones Industrial Average surpassed 1,000 for the first time in history—what some felt was an "astronomical level." Frankly, it's hard to recall anything that long ago, but the one thing I do remember is that nobody in the fall of 1962 was advising people to buy stocks or to take any kind of shot at the market. In retrospect that's what everyone should have done. What was present was one of the greatest buying opportunities that I've been fortunate enough to have lived through.

Ten years later, 1972, saw a similar situation. Stock prices had been low, the economy was bad, and things looked bleak. Then lo and behold on one bright day the stock market, as measured by the Dow Jones Industrial Average, began to rally. As is usually the case, the savants and sages of Wall Street did not herald in this buy point. However, 1972 was not quite like 1962, a point that needs to be fixed in every investor's mind. Seldom is one rally or year exactly like the prior period. Although there was a tremendous rally in the fall of 1972, it quickly gave way to a decline in 1973 and 1974 before the next substantial bull market began.

My search for stock market truth, which began in 1962, included an interesting selection of books, among them *Tides in the Affairs of Men* by Anthony Gaubis and Edgar Lawrence Smith (Macmillan, 1939). These authors' central point was that there is a 10-year pattern in the U.S. stock

market and economy. The thrust of their argument was that most stock
market highs come in the latter part of every decade. By that they meant
that one was more likely to find stock market highs in years ending in six
and nine, such as 1966 and 1929. Gaubis and Smith looked at the cycle
going back into the earlier part of the 1900s and presented their case in
the book.

As a young man I simply had no perspective, as well as very little confidence that this long-range pattern (or cycle) really worked. I wondered if
it would hold in the future. I did not know this then, but I sure do now.
While certainly the 10-year pattern has not precisely called all major market highs and lows, it has done a very, very good job of pointing investors
to the most probable, logical, and best times for the stock market to rally
or decline.

The ensuing years have given me much to think about as I have studied
the markets and economic cycles. As an example, the stock market debacles we saw in the latter part of the twentieth century occurred in synch
with what Gaubis and Smith wrote; stocks got slammed in 1987, as well as
1989. And of course, the one no one will ever forget: 1999 was the top for
the Nasdaq's high-flying stocks and the beginning of a 76 percent correction in high-tech issues.—a correction that wiped out many individual investors, professionals, and mutual funds.

Was it possible that the decennial pattern identified, at least in part, the
economic up-and-down swings from 1962 forward? It is an interesting
question, one I will address in this book and one I think, after you see the
data, you will agree presents a superb buying opportunity for 2002 and
2005. I am deeply indebted to Gaubis and Smith for starting my journey
on the path of looking for stock market cycles. Unlike many students of
market cycles, though, quite frankly I don't place much value on most of
them. For sure, I do not think they are precise. Most market cycles, such as
the 18-day cycle, 200-day cycle, and all that, are at best difficult to trade or
use to invest. Yet there are several very dominant cycles that seem to hold
water, and more importantly, hold up in the future. That's what much of
this book is about.

Additionally, I'd like to share with you some methods, ideas, and
techniques of investing I have discovered and found to be successful for
the average investor. These are easy to use and easy to follow. They can
and do get to the heart and truth of the markets. It does not matter what
a company does in terms of its product or service nearly as much as
whether the company is profitable and what its growth prospects are.

That was a problem with the roaring bull market of high-tech stocks: Fundamentally they were not sound, so while stories carried them to some amazing price levels, they couldn't maintain those levels. That they would crash was inevitable.

What I hope to show you is that fundamentals have moved stocks in the past and will move stocks in the future, regardless of what the company does. Ultimately, it always gets down the fundamentals; it always gets down to value. As the great baseball manager Tommy Lasorda said, "God may delay but God does not deny." In this business of speculating, value in the form of growth and profitability may indeed be overlooked for a while, but ultimately it prevails.

In 1982, I wrote a book called *How to Prosper in the Coming Good Years*. It was a refutation of the negativity the purveyors of pessimism had spread across the country at that time. I took an outrageously bullish posture on the future for two reasons. First, Ronald Reagan and supply-side economics were coming on the scene. My study of the past showed that every time we had such incentive-based economic programs and incentive-oriented economic systems, the markets always went higher.

On top of this was one simple fact that had been hanging in the cobwebs of my mind since 1962: Years ending in two usually produced the start of bull markets . . . years ending in twos usually produced overall economic up terms. So this book is very much a continuation of that 1982 book. The greatness of our economic system lies in front of us, not behind us. It is not all over; the good times are coming now as they will continue in the future. This book aims to help you pinpoint when those times are most apt to occur.

I would like to personally welcome you into my world of speculation, into the art of divining the future, into the art of living not in the past but in the tomorrows in today's be-here-now world.

LARRY WILLIAMS

Rancho Santa Fe, California
February 2003

THE RIGHT STOCK
AT THE RIGHT TIME

1

THE 10-YEAR PATTERN IN THE UNITED STATES STOCK MARKET

"It's about time."
—My U.S. senatorial campaign slogan, 1978

What did the fall 2002 buying opportunity really mean? Are more fortune-making buy points coming in 2005, 2006, 2007, and 2008?

In this book I will go into detail explaining what I think will be the best buy points over the next 10 years. That's quite a claim. Can it be done, and if so how?

I'd like to first catch your attention with this: If one were to look for the best buying points of the twentieth century one could not help but notice that these stellar opportunities came in 1903, 1912, 1913, and 1920 into 1923. The ultimate best buy point came in 1932. This was followed by wonderful buy points in 1942, 1952, and 1962; 1972 wasn't bad (though 1973 was better), and, of course, 1982 was perhaps the second best buy point of the twentieth century. That was followed by another superb buy point in 1992. Notice that for the past 100 years, these ideal buying points came in years ending with a two or a three.

If you had invested in just these years you would have substantially outperformed the investor who chose to continually buy stocks. I find this rather amazing and, better yet, to be hard evidence that indeed there's something going on in the U.S. stock market—something that shows us when the best buying opportunities tend to occur. They are usually to be found in the first part of the decade—namely, years ending in twos and threes.

Figures 1.1 through 1.6 are of historic stock market activity and are well worth your study. The first, the Axe-Houghton index of stock market averages from 1854 until 1935, is from my personal files. The next group of figures, from Moore Research Centers, Inc., shows price activity for the 101 years from 1900 to 2001.

THE PAST IS THE FUTURE

The 1800s were no different from the 1900s; they presented a very similar scenario. Stocks roared in 1862 and 1872; 1883 was very close to a wonderful buy point, which came in early 1884. Along came 1893, which presented another good buying opportunity. I do not mean to imply that all one has to do as an investor is buy stocks every 10 years. I wish it were that easy! But it certainly helps to have a concept and time zone of when one wants to make a major play in the stock market. My concept of this is that years ending in twos and threes are most likely to turn out to be gargantuan buying points. It is almost as simple as that.

THE ROAD MAP TO MARKET SUCCESS

As a very young man, I followed the work of Edson Gould, who published an advisory service called "Finding and Forecasts." How I wish I had paid more attention to what Edson had to say. While it is true he had many arcane forms of forecasting, he consistently relied on the action of the Federal Reserve Board and what he called the 10-year pattern for stock prices.

Although I did not know it at the time, I'd been handed, figuratively speaking, the keys to the kingdom of stock market forecasting. The irony of the situation is that I spent the next seven years trying to determine how to forecast stock market prices out into the future. I studied the works of W. D. Gann as well as those of R. N. Elliott, several leading astrologers, and so on, which all turned out to be a waste of time. I was fortunate enough to eventually meet Gann's son, who was a broker in New York City and who explained to me that his father was simply a chartist. He asked why, if his dad was good as everyone said, the son was still "smiling and dialing," calling up customers to trade." It seemed he was somewhat disturbed by his father's

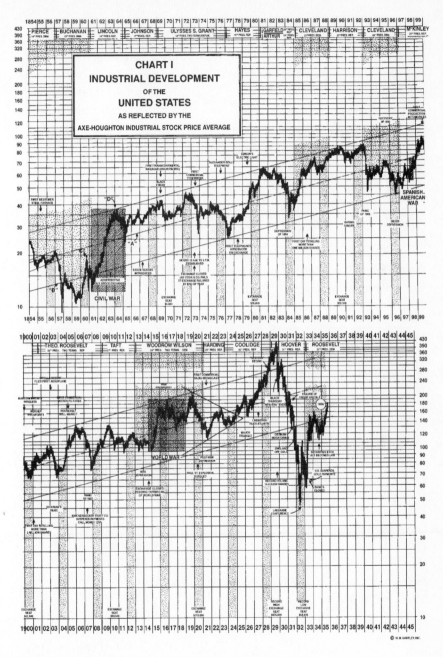

Figure 1.1 Market Averages from 1854 to 1935

Source: Axe-Houghton.

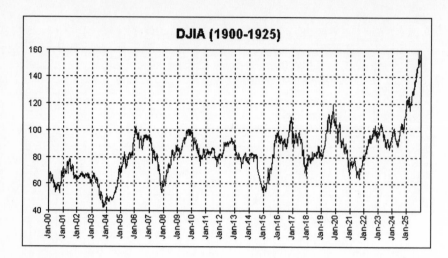

Figure 1.2   Dow Jones Industrial Average, 1900–1925
Source: Moore Research Center, Inc.

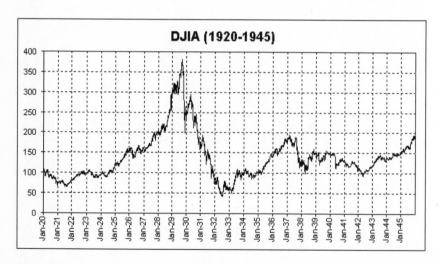

Figure 1.3   Dow Jones Industrial Average, 1920–1945
Source: Moore Research Center, Inc.

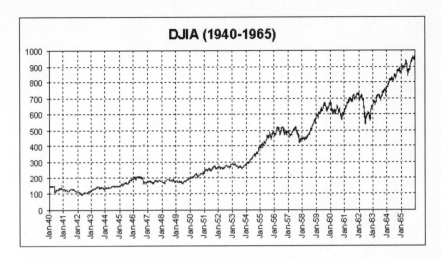

Figure 1.4   Dow Jones Industrial Average, 1940–1965
Source: Moore Research Center, Inc.

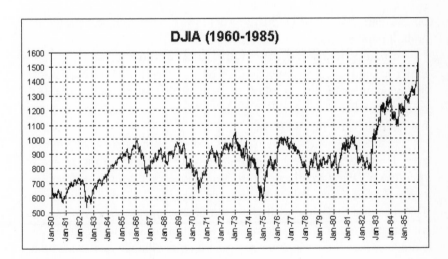

Figure 1.5   Dow Jones Industrial Average, 1960–1985
Source: Moore Research Center, Inc.

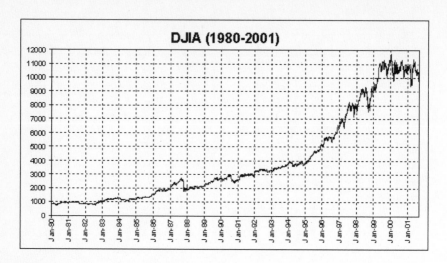

Figure 1.6   Dow Jones Industrial Average, 1980–2001
Source: Moore Research Center, Inc.

press-agentry, as it had led many people to come to him seeking the holy grail. If there was one, it was never passed on to the son.

At that same time I also met F. B. Thatcher, who had been Gann's promoter and advance man. He assured me in correspondence over the last five years of his life that in fact Gann was just a good promoter, not necessarily a good stock trader. F.B. made his own predictions, and they were not bad, but certainly not great.

He did give me his version of the genesis of the legend of Gann as a great forecaster. It all began, he told me, with an article in the *Ticker and Investment Digest* that has been reprinted many times since, where it was reported that Gann sold wheat at the high tick, or price, of the day. Thatcher said they simply hired a good press agent to place the story in a magazine for them. The magazine article placement was accomplished over a dinner where there was some pretty serious drinking as well some money sliding under the table, along with payment for a large ad in the magazine.

I did not know any of this at the time I began my search for something to predict the future. Like everyone else, I believed what I had read about all the great predictors. I wish now I had just stayed with the forecasting techniques that Gould devised. His techniques have been not only more accurate than Gann's but also a heck of a lot simpler to follow.

Figure 1.7 is just as presented by Gould as well as shown in Yale

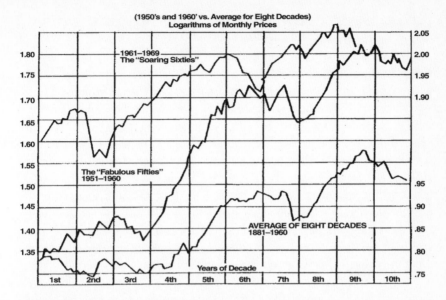

Figure 1.7　Ten-Year Patterns of Industrial Stock Prices

Sources: 1881–1917, Cowles Commission Industrials; 1918–1969, Standard & Poors's 425 Industrial Stock Price Index.

Reprinted from Yale Hirsch, *Don't Sell Stocks on Monday*.

Hirsch's book, *Don't Sell Stocks on Monday* (Facts on File Publications, 1986). The bottom line of the chart traces the average of eight decades of market history from 1881 to 1960.

Gould had taken the time to average, by hand, stock prices from 1881 through 1960 on a monthly basis. In this day and age, we can do that in almost the blink of an eye with a computer. I'm certain it took Gould a good year of work. Essentially, what he did was to average every month from 1881 forward through 1960. By this I mean he compared all January price movements in those 80 years to all other Januarys. This created a pattern that Gould used as a general road map that he expected the stock market to follow. What is fascinating is that while his work was completed in 1960, the roaring bull market of the 1960s fit the pattern almost to a T. Then along came the sluggish 1970s, and again the markets moved pretty much in accordance with the road map. The 1980s seemed to an almost uncanny extent to follow the road map Gould had charted out for us, with the crash of 1987 coming exactly where Gould's forecasts said it would occur. The tremendous buying point of late 1987 and early 1988 also was represented on the chart he made in 1960. I find that most remarkable.

Even more startling is that the end of the Nasdaq run-up in the waning weeks of the twentieth century also came in the tenth year of the decade, where Gould postulated market tops are most likely to be found.

The chart shown here reflects Gould's work using the Cowles Commission Industrials from 1881 to 1917; that stock market index was then blended into the Standard & Poor's index from 1918 to 1969. As you can see, his work suggests that the first year of a decade, such as 1981, 1991, and 2001, presents investors with choppy to down markets. Sometimes markets take off in years ended in two, such as 1982 or 1932; and for sure by the time the third year rolls around, such as 1983 or 1993, a bull market begins. I would suggest you place this road map of prices in your safe-deposit box to give your children instead of an inheritance. It has more value, and I don't think the value will deflate over the coming inflationary time periods.

Figure 1.8, thanks to Moore Research, shows what we call "out-of-sample" data. This means the chart reflects information not in the original time under study. In short, an idea or conclusion is reached from observing one time period; then the thesis is applied to data from another time, either before or after the test or discovery period. Seldom does the idea work on the out-of-sample information, by the way.

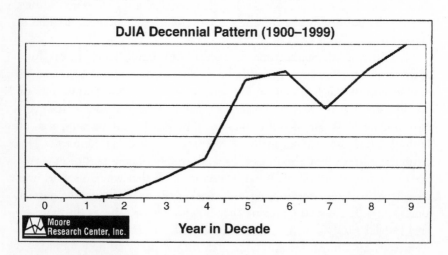

Figure 1.8   Dow Jones Industrial Average Decennial Pattern, 1900–1999
Source: Moore Research Center, Inc.

In this case we averaged the 1980s and the 1990s to continue the same procedure used by Gould on the earlier data. The pattern holds, telling us there is consistency to the concept. What we see is that in the card game of the future pretty much the same cards were dealt as in the past.

Let me tell you how unusual this is. Of the many trading systems and strategies I have developed in some 40 years of trading, the vast majority perform at about 40 percent efficiency after the test. In other words, one should not expect a repeat performance very often. The reality is that once a system or technique is run on unknown data, seldom does it hold up or come even close to what the original study showed.

In the summer of 2001, when I began writing this book, it seemed fairly clear to me that I was looking at a road map that pointed to some type of buying point coming in the mid to latter part of 2002 as well as in late 2003. In lectures across the United States I told investors what I saw as a rare opportunity to buy stocks.

Figure 1.9 shows what happened after Gould's chart was published: The pattern of stock prices for 1881 to 1960 continued. Figure 1.7 has already shown that the roaring bull market of the 1950s and 1960s fit the pattern quite closely, and Figure 1.8 superimposed the 1980s as well as 1990s over the basic forecast made some 40 years ago.

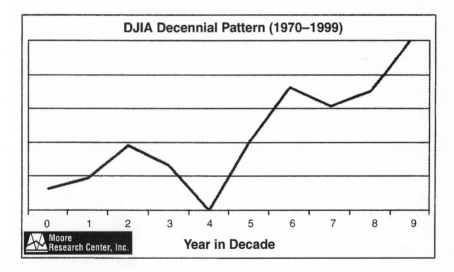

Figure 1.9   Dow Jones Industrial Average Decennial Pattern, 1970–1999
Source: Moore Research Center, Inc.

It does not matter whether you have been following the markets for 30 years or 30 minutes; you can see that there is more than "just an interesting pattern" at work here. Far from it; what you are looking at is the ultimate insight as to the road stock prices are most apt to follow. Indeed, for over 150 years there has been a consistent ebb and flow of stock prices based on the start and finish of each decade. Note, this is not a 10-year pattern; its basis is the beginning and ending of each decade. To that extent, 10 years of data are observed, but it is not a 10-year cycle.

As a longtime observer of market activity I can tell you there is nothing on the face of this planet that has a better record of giving us the general time periods to be bullish and bearish than the way stock prices have on average carved an upward course each decade in a steady fashion.

THE "PHENOMENAL FIVE" YEARS

I have learned a lot about the markets from my longtime good friend Yale Hirsch (all he learned from me was how to catch trout). Yale has also uncovered a second important point within this overall pattern of price swings. Yale pointed out in his book *Don't Sell Stocks on Monday* that the middle year of this 10-year pattern tends to produce some real rock-and-roll upside markets. Table 1.1 shows the average gain of each individual year of the decade. At the time his book was written we had 11 decades under our belt for study. What we see is that in 11 out of 11 times the fifth year in the decade produced a rally or a market-up move, making it the strongest year in the 10-year pattern. Years ending in eight showed winners in 8 out of 10 occurrences. The poorer-performing years were those ending in seven and those years ending in a zero, as the Edgar Lawrence Smith's work had suggested.

That is well and good, but of greater importance to an investor is *how much* money was made in a year, not simply whether the year was up or down. Without a doubt the fifth years of the decades have been where the bulk of wealth has been made. Yale's work showed a total gain of 254 percent in the five years, making them head and shoulders above even the second-place eight years, which came in with a 164 percent gain.

What Yale had no way of knowing was what would happen in the 1990s. It was unknown at that time how 1995 would perform.

Table 1.1 The 10-Year Stock Market Cycle: Annual Percent Change in Standard & Poor's Composite Index Past 100 Years

Decade	\multicolumn{10}{c}{Year of Decade}

Decade	1st	2nd	3rd	4th	5th	6th	7th	8th	9th	10th
1881–1890	—	—	—	—	20	9	−7	−2	3	−14
1891–1900	18	1	−20	−3	1	−2	13	19	7	14
1901–1910	16	1	−19	25	16	3	−33	37	14	−12
1911–1920	1	3	−14	−9	32	3	−31	16	13	−24
1921–1930	7	20	−3	19	23	5	26	36	−15	−29
1931–1940	−47	−18	48	−2	39	28	−34	13	0	−12
1941–1950	−15	6	21	14	33	−10	−2	−2	11	20
1951–1960	15	7	−3	39	23	4	−13	33	11	−4
1961–1970	27	−13	18	13	9	−11	17	12	−14	−1
1971–1980	10	12	−19	−32	32	18	−10	2	11	26
1981–1990	−7	13	18	0	26	—	—	—	—	—
Up years	7	8	4	6	11	7	3	8	8	3
Down years	3	2	6	4	0	3	7	2	2	7
Total % change	25%	32%	27%	64%	254%	47%	−74%	164%	41%	−36%

Based on average December prices.

Would it follow this tradition? Or would it break the consecutive string of the 11 winning years ending in a five? And how about that eight year in the pattern—would it also produce gains similar to those as it had in the past?

Years ending in a five from 1885 through 1985 had produced an average gain of 23 percent; years ending in an eight had produced an average gain of 14.9 percent. Keep in mind that the 1881–1990 data shows a total gain of 254 percent for the fifth year, or an average of 19.5 percent per year.

The year 1995 produced a spectacular gain of 33.5 percent by the Dow Jones Industrial Average while 1998 produced a gain of 14.9 percent, making these the two best-performing years of the 1990s. Just think, the gains of 1995 and 1998 were right on schedule according to the pattern detected generations earlier. Keep in mind that forecast was essentially locked into iron shackles in 1960, yet was able to correctly point investors to the two most profitable years in the 1990–2000 bull market.

Perhaps, just perhaps, the stock market is a little bit easier to understand than you ever thought.

I suggest you take a great deal of time to look at and restudy the longer-term charts presented in this book in order to get a sense of this phenomenon and perhaps pick up the cadence at which the market moves.

THE "SURE THING SEVEN" YEARS

Clearly, some years are better for buying than others. The focus of my work has been to ferret out the best years, the most explosive, the ones with the greatest odds of having significant upside action. Sure, you can buy and hold for 20 years and make money—no brilliance there. What I want is to make my wagers when the dice are loaded.

The addition to our knowledge of the 10-year pattern means that there is yet one more place to look to buy stocks. Is it just coincidence that the 1960 road map, which suggested a major buy point at the end of any year ending in seven, scored with big wins in 1977, 1987, and 1997? Each of those years provided investors with excellent end-of-year buy points. I suspect it is not just coincidence. I suspect there is something going on in the general economy or business cycle—call it what you may—because this pattern is simply repeated too many times, too often, to be just some random fluctuation of numbers.

It's now time for you to restudy the Axe-Houghton index of stock prices from 1854 forward (Figure 1.1). The same phenomenon can be found to occur: In late 1857 stocks bottomed, then almost doubled in price. The fall of 1867 produced an equally spectacular rally that continued all the way to the 1869 market high.

Wouldn't you know it? When 1877 rolled around, stocks again bottomed about midyear, and then later in the year a two-year bull market began. That takes us to 1887, when again, in the fall of the year, stock prices bottomed before beginning a two-and-a-half-year bull move.

The year 1897 saw pretty much the same thing: Prices bottomed early in the year, followed by a summer run-up, a pullback in the fall of the year (the seven year buy zone), and then another two-year bull market. The 1907 bottom came late in the year, about December, just before another two-year bull market. The year 1917 was almost a replica of 1907; again prices got hammered at the end of that year before they took off on another two-year bull market.

Then there's 1927. What more can one say? There appears to be no major low here—prices went straight up. But if you look closely you see in the fall of 1927 where prices stabilized briefly, pulling back off the year's high before another two-year bull market surged to the 1929 top.

Well, that brings us to the Moore Research data and 1937, a year stocks declined with a vengeance, bottoming in the first of quarter 1938 before another two-year bull market began. (This time the seven year phenomenon was off by about three months.) In fact, that's pretty much what happened 10 years later in 1947, when the average moved sideways most of the year, came down in the fall, and bottomed in mid-February 1948. No two-year bull market followed, though; prices simply had a huge, one-year run-up in 1948.

In 1957 stocks followed the model perfectly. There was a run-up in the first part of 1957; prices then crashed coming into an October low or a bottom, to begin one more substantial up move in the U.S. stock market. This was in perfect harmony with the seventh-year price pattern.

Ten years later yet one more wonderful buy point was presented. Stocks rallied during the first part of 1967, then took a tumble into the fall of that year, bottoming in February 1968 and starting not a two-year bull market, but a strong rally for the rest of 1968. Clearly, history shows there was a very nice buy point in late 1967 and early 1968.

Does it appear to you there is something to this phenomenon? It does to me. Is there an explanation for it? I can come up with some explanations, but I'm not certain they prove a point any more convincingly than a study of the five years and the seven years as well as the two and three years in terms of historical precedent. The charts don't lie. The phenomenon is there, and it's up to us to learn how to exploit the past so our investments might be better in the future.

Of course what we're talking about here is just timing. We still have to get into the issue of selection—what stocks to buy. However, most investors have a pretty good idea of companies they want to purchase; they just don't know the right time to do so. Buying or selling at the right time does make a huge difference. As an example, on balance, if you purchased stocks at the start of the sixth year of the decade, you had to wait only until the eighth year to make money. *If you purchased stocks in the years ending in nine, you had to wait almost five years, on average, before your stock showed a profit.* So timing your entries and exits in the stock market is critical. I believe following the 10-year price pattern is one way to gain an advantage in this business of speculation.

It would seem unreasonable to expect stock prices to follow some mythical and perhaps even mystical road map observed in the 1960s on out into eternity. Yet, that is precisely what has taken place, by and large, which raises the question, will markets of the twenty-first century continue to follow this road map? That is a question that will not be answered until the time period is over. However, we can watch during the first 10 years, from 2001 to 2010, to see how closely this pattern is repeated. I suspect that it will be repeated, and more closely than you might imagine. The acid test comes sometime after 2005. If 2005 is another rip-roaring bull market year and the overall price pattern follows the 10-year road map, I think it will give even more validity to this concept and investors should have more confidence in using it as a general guideline of investment activity for years, or perhaps decades, to come.

The market appears to have repetitive tendencies to how it unfolds over the years. The frame of reference does indeed seem to be the decennial pattern. Within that framework there are particular times that one should look for optimal buy (and sell) points.

The first would be years ending in twos and threes, followed by the incredibly strong five years. The next opportunity to look for a buy point is in the fall of any year ending in seven.

Finally, a long-term investor should never forget that most major market highs have come in years ending in nine and zero, such as 1929, 1969, 1999, and of course 2000.

I look upon this decennial pattern as the most logical road map that prices will follow. I certainly do not expect prices to match this price pattern precisely each year, or each decade. It wouldn't be any fun to trade stocks if it were that easy. But we are given excellent guidelines here of which turns in the road to take, as well as when to take them.

2

THE FOUR-YEAR PHENOMENON

Future wealth is purchased with scrutiny of the past.

Thanks to the writings of Edson Gould, Edgar Lawrence Smith, Anthony Gaubis, and Yale Hirsch, we have a pretty good idea of when to expect significant stock market highs and lows within the decennial pattern. It is a wonderful general road map of what is most likely to happen in the future and alerts us to each decade's fifth and seventh year buying opportunities. But we need something more specific. After all, we all want to know not only the precise week or day but also the exact time of day to buy or sell our stock. I think that's a stretch, but with various market tools we *can* get a whole lot closer to determining the best time to buy or sell.

The next bit of market knowledge I'd like to share with you is something I stumbled across in 1970 that is the next key ingredient in my forecast for 2002. The bear market of 1970 had been good to me. I'd made my first so-called killing in the markets, about $300,000—not much now, but back then it counted to a 28-year-old kid, and gave me a hefty dose of a young man's cockiness.

My attitude of being so smart as to find the bear market and sell it short also convinced me to stay short after the low. I gave some of the money back, and was still nibbling on the short side in October of that year when stocks rallied through the roof. Ouch! That hurt the pride as well as the pocketbook.

I eventually wised up and went long. Late one night as I was licking my wounds and staring at old charts, I saw something that changed my entire perspective on longer-term timing.

What I noticed on my charts was the four-year space from the low of 1962 to 1966 to 1970. That got me to wondering whether there was some repetitive pattern at work here that no one had told me about. My father always advised me that what little success I would have in life would be due more to hard work and luck than intelligence. With that thought in mind I began poring over all the old charts I had collected.

And there it was: Going back in time from 1962 there had been an important market low four years earlier, in 1958! That got me excited, so I next looked back four more years to 1954 and there it was—the start of another bull market. By now my heart was pumping. Had I found something here? What happened in 1950? It was back to the charts and back to the start of another bull market.

I was impressed! But it didn't make sense to me that we would have market lows with such repetitive accuracy. What's more, why didn't they teach me this stuff in college or why hadn't I read about it in a book? I had never seen this in print. It was a sleepless night for me—I couldn't stop thinking about the powerful effect of market low after market low every four years. It was one of those things that just seemed too good to be true. Was it possible this phenomenon would work in the future?

FEAR SETS IN

Market information of this nature plays tricks with one's thinking. I had pretty well proven, to my satisfaction, the power of the four-year phenomenon—but then reasoned that if I knew it, then it would not work in the future. On top of that, my reactive mind added the idea that I needed more examples out of the great unknown of the future to validate my discovery.

So I waited with fear and trepidation, hoping no one knew my "dirty little secret," to see how this four-year "whatever it was" would pan out in the future. Along came the market low of 1974, and again in 1978 there was a decent buy point, considering the stagnant market we had been in.

I had now collected two out-of-sample instances of the phenomenon. In some uncanny way stocks had continued bottoming in phase with this four-year cycle.

If that's all you knew about the stock market back in 1978 you would have been waiting for the next buy point to come four years later in 1982. And that is exactly when the longest-lasting bull market in the history of mankind began. Add four years to 1982 and you get 1986 as our next projection. Even a cursory glance of the charts shows yet another wonderful buy point in the fall of that year.

My confidence in this phenomenon had increased to a marked degree. To think that observations made in 1970 were still having tremendous market success 16 years later was proof to me of the validity of what I had seen late that night when I was licking my wounds from being bearish too long. Necessity is certainly the mother of invention.

Figures 2.1A and 2.1B, again from Moore Research, break market activity down to give you a better view of what has taken place from 1900 forward. I have marked off the four-year phenomena and low points for you on the charts. I ogle these charts like a 14-year-old boy eyeballs his first copy of *Playboy* magazine. They can greatly add to your

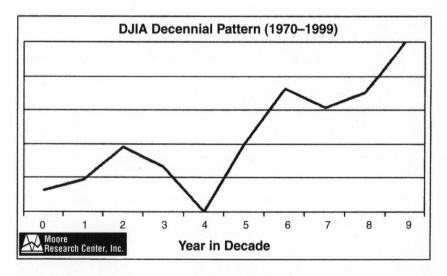

Figure 2.1A   Dow Jones Industrial Average Decennial Pattern 1970–1999
Source: Moore Research Center, Inc.

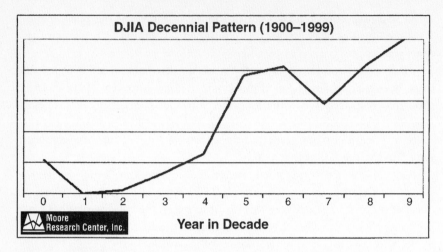

Figure 2.1B Dow Jones Industrial Average Decennial Pattern 1900–1999
Source: Moore Research Center, Inc.

understanding of major cyclical moves and help you build confidence on your own so you can take action when the time is right.

SO EASY A KID CAN DO IT

This four-year phenomenon is so simple that even a kid can do it! We simply add four years to the October buy point in 1986, and our imaginary 14-year-old kid can expect to call for a market low in the fall of 1990. At the ripe old age of 18 he watches a year-and-a-half bull market begin. Imagine—we have kids beating the pros with a market timing system so easy to follow all it needs is four fingers. Throw away the rocket-science math, and leave your laptop at home—you don't need a computer!

Our hypothetical kid investor now adds four years to the low in 1990 and makes this outrageous forecast that stocks should bottom in the fall of 1994. He's not a kid any longer—he's now 22, and beats the pants off the Wall Street experts when in the fall of that year one of the most dramatic price increases mankind has ever seen begins, an exponential rally similar to that leading to the high in 1929. Not only does the Dow Jones Industrial Average go up, but virtually everything rallies—junk stocks, tech stocks, blue chips, small caps. Everyone makes money following the kid investor's forecast to buy stocks in 1994.

As our kid investor approaches the ripe old age of 26 he's looking for another market bottom four years after the one in 1994. He has made a killing in the ensuing market rally, so he's got plenty of cash to plunk into a market buying opportunity. Fortunately, he did not go to Harvard Business School, or the Wharton School of Finance. He's smart enough not to listen to analysts, watch financial programs on television, or read the *Wall Street Journal*. He just has this thing about every four years there should be a market bottom.

Our hypothetical investor is a little perplexed once 1998 rolls around. By now he is aware that the vast majority of analysts are calling for a major stock market crash. He kind of thinks that might happen as well (because every four years he has seen early and midyear weakness leading to a low). In the summer of that year prices take a terrible beating. Many investors think this is the slide that in reality would come two years later. The air is thick with bearishness; you can slice it with a knife in October 1998. That is precisely when our rapidly maturing kid investor decides to belly up to the bar and buy stocks one more time. The entry point is simple; it is four years after his 1994 wealth-making foray in the marketplace.

His ignorance or lack of market understanding, college degrees, and all that pays off in spades as stocks begin another 18 months of an almost vertical market rally. His timing could not have been more impeccable! Once more our inexperienced, uneducated, but by now fabulously wealthy kid investor has hit it right on the button.

He has done what the pros—the fund managers, brokers, and investment advisers—were not able to do. He outsmarted them all with his annual four-year forecast.

THE MEANING OF 2002

Let's see if we can get this straight now; every four years we expect a market bottom. The last one was in 1998, so if we simply add four years to 1998 we should then expect the next buying opportunity. If my math is correct, 1998 plus four more years calls for a major buying opportunity in 2002. Since the 1998 low came in October of 1998, I would expect a market low to occur about the same time of year—the fall of 2002.

That is from the original manuscript written for this book in the fall of 2001. Sure enough, the 2002 buy point came. But was this just a rally in a bear market? The history of these four-year buys suggests to me that 2002 was a major buy area, not just a bleep before a crash to lower price levels.

Incidentally, one should also be looking for significant market bottoms in 2006, 2010, 2014, 2018, 2022, 2026, 2030, 2034, 2038, 2042, 2046, and 2050.

There it is, my forecast for the next 50 years of market activity. Many things will happen in the next 50 years. There will be huge changes in society, in business, in communications, even religion and politics, yet I suspect the four-year phenomenon will continue to be the clockwork of the marketplace.

I say that not because this four-year phenomenon has done such an exceptionally good job of forecasting prices from 1962 forward, but because it also did such a good job of forecasting prices prior to 1962.

One of my studies was to do a count of this cycle for all years of market activity from 1858 forward. I found that 86 percent of the time stocks bottomed in perfect harmony with this four-year repetitive pattern. Accuracy like this is extremely difficult to find in the stock market, and certainly suggests that something beyond random activity is involved. The mere fact that the four-year phenomenon has been so influential for so many years suggests rather strongly to me that it will continue performing for many years yet to come. It is ironic to think that something as simplistic as this four-year pattern has done a better job of calling major market lows than virtually any of the fancy indicators and investment strategies we have cooked up with elaborate mathematics and econometric models.

Some people suspect this has something to do with the presidential election cycle, which does neatly dovetail with this four-year phenomenon. Others I have shared it with think it has something to do with the planet Mars (I have eclectic friends). Some say it is part of the decennial pattern. The very few people who know of this pattern seem to think it may be a natural cyclical response to human activity or is perhaps somehow influenced by Federal Reserve activity.

I really don't know. I can come up with some conclusions and reasons to explain why the phenomenon occurs, but does it make a difference? The facts speak rather well for themselves. The market has had way too many bottoms coming in way too often at the right time for me to monkey around much with the data. I would rather just accept it. What is, is. To me it's as simple as that.

142 YEARS OF MARKET SUCCESS

I have stock market prices as far back as 1854 (shown in Chapter 1). It appears this four-year phenomenon began operating in 1858, when the market was close to an important low (which actually came in 1859). The next indication was four years later, in 1862, early in one of the strongest bull markets of the entire century. Fast-forward to 1866, where we can find a low point established in the fall of that year marking the beginning of a two-and-a-half-year bull market.

You know the drill; we add four years to 1866 and come up with 1870 as a buy point in the stock market, which was exactly on target (Michael Jordan was never more accurate). Four more years produces 1874, which did start a nice up move into 1875, eventually leading to one of those long-lasting bull moves investors dream of. Our next buy zone would, of course, be 1878, which was a spectacular one in that the equity market danced to the bull's tunes in perfect synchronization with our four-year phenomenon.

This of course meant we would next be looking for a buying opportunity in 1882. This one did not work at all; prices continued going down until 1884. However, any money lost at that buy point, and certainly an investor would have used stop-loss orders, was recouped four years later as 1886 heralded in another bull market than did not culminate until 1893.

Our next four-year phenomenon buy point was scheduled for 1890. Interestingly enough the fall of that year did present a wonderful buy point for a bull market that lasted into the winter of 1893. Again, the four-year phenomenon scored a major victory. The averages rallied.

The next call was for a low in 1894. This one was a bit premature. Yes, prices did rally off the low of the year of 1894, but the real market low came in 1896. Our patient investor awaited the next buying opportunity to occur in 1898. That patience was rewarded in substantial investment gains as the market took off once more in line with our four-year phenomenon.

Oh-oh, the turn of the century had taken place! Could, and would, this handy dandy little pattern work in both centuries? It would suggest to our investor back then to purchase stocks in 1902, four years after the 1898 buy point. Unfortunately this turning point was not so spectacular—prices did rally late in that year but came down rather sharply in 1903. Four years later we would have looked to step in again on the long side as a buyer in 1906. Our reward? Failure.

The year 1910 would have presented the next opportunity to see if stock prices were moving in phase with the four-year phenomenon. Given the prior two misses, I'm sure we would have been shaking in our boots, wondering if this phenomenon had started to falter—because while prices did rally this time it took awhile and there certainly was no spectacular up move.

Then, in gangbuster-like fashion, the four-year phenomenon started to click in like digital clockwork; a market low came in 1914, 1918, 1922, and 1926. None appeared in 1930, but market lows reappeared in 1934, 1938, 1942, 1946, 1950, 1954, 1958, 1962, and on to the present. Four years after four years, in an almost robotlike fashion, the phenomenon kicked in, working as well in the second 100 years as it had in the first.

Clearly one can learn from the past. The lesson that I see here is to expect stock market lows in harmony with the four-year phenomenon. The market low in 2002 (1998 + 4) just so happens to coincide with the decennial road map forecast for an important market low in the 2002–2003 time period.

In other words, we have a kind of double confirmation here—both major long-term cyclical reference frames are telling us to expect an up move in stock prices at this time. While the decennial pattern is somewhat general, we can most definitely focus or narrow our window of opportunity to a substantial degree in synch with the four-year phenomenon pattern, thus isolating the best of the best.

As an aside, we can also see, in that sense, a market bottom is called for by the four-year phenomenon in 2006, four years after the 2002 low, which dovetails with our fifth year decennial pattern scenario. This suggests to me that not only will the stock market rally in 2005 but that a buy point will be found in 2006 as well, thus indicating that some type of substantial rally in stock prices is out there for us to take advantage of.

Even better may be the 2014 market low that is expected thanks to the four-year phenomenon, which then leads into the fifth year expected rally in 2015. Should you and I both be so lucky as to still be trading at that time, you know which side of the market I'll be on, and you know I will have covered my short sales.

The use of the decennial pattern as well as my four-year phenomenon is not some conjecture on my part, some bit of numerology applied to stock prices. Twenty years ago an earlier book of mine touched on this subject. In 1981, while standing at a supermarket checkout counter, I noticed the then best-selling book *How to Prosper in the Coming Bad Years* by Howard Ruff. It struck me that what investors needed was a dose of good old-fashioned optimism; it was time for a new book, a new view of the economy. *How to Prosper in the Coming Good Years* was my response to the purveyors of pessimism.

To a large degree that book, with its bullish view, was based on what I've discussed so far. I knew the decennial pattern should kick in for a low in 1982 or 1983. I also knew that my four-year phenomenon was calling for a low at the same time as the decennial pattern.

As the book promotion began in the winter of 1982 things looked very bleak. Most of the folks who interviewed me were shocked by my optimism, by my predictions of good times to come, and by my panning of the pessimists.

The most notable experiences were on the Merv Griffin show, an interview by Dan Dorfman, and a never-to-be-forgotten radio talk show in Detroit.

The talk show was supposed to last 30 minutes. It began with a brief introduction, my expression of extreme optimism that good times would come and rather quickly. Then we went to the phone lines; they lit up like a Fourth of July night. The callers to this station were upset and angry with me for being so optimistic. They did not want to argue or discuss the political or economic situation, reasons why things might get better; they simply wanted to shout and scream, taking out their frustrations on my optimism. Investors had just lost a lot of money in the 1970s market. It was no wonder; stocks had been down to sideways for years, inflation had been rampant during Jimmy Carter's tour of duty, and investors—even those who bought and held gold—had little to show in the way of profits.

For a long time, long-term investors had only losses to show for their efforts and risk. This condition breeds disbelief and contempt for bull markets. Such a condition is exactly what sets up the opportunity for major buy points. Why? Most investors think the coming six months to a year will be pretty much like the prior six months to a year. They are overly influenced by the current trend; they are looking back, not forward.

The 30-minute interview opened up to a three-hour telethon that Jerry Lewis would have been proud of. People just could not accept the idea that things might get better, that perhaps the future of America was bright, not dim.

In retrospect this was one of the all-time market calls. Wherever I went throughout the United States, some 32 cities in 28 days, my message was clear: "Mortgage your house, buy stocks, then get a second mortgage and buy more."

Here we are 20 years later—entering a year two and year three time frame with a four-year phenomenon kicking in at the same market juncture.

THE "STRAIGHT EIGHT" FACTOR

While I have pointed out a year seven low point phenomenon, there's another part to this cycle or pattern that is important.

Simply stated, it's this: Years ending in two and eight have shown a unique ability to start major market rallies. Usually this begins in the first three months of that year. It is almost as though the year seven low point, such as the one presented to investors in 1987, gets so oversold, or perhaps undervalued, that prices have easy sailing for the next year, the one ending in an eight.

Again, I'm not certain why this phenomenon exists. Some say it is due to sun spots; some say barometric pressure; I'd say Federal Reserve activity. While there's plenty of room for discussion about the cause of this phenomenon, there can be no discussion about whether it exists.

In researching prices back to 1850 I noted that there have been 15 times we have seen this pattern appear. That means we have 150 years of experience with this intriguing year eight opportunity, which I think you'll find presents a superb buying opportunity.

Some of the most exponential moves in the entire history of the stock market are those that started with years ending in an eight, such as 1888, 1928, 1938, and no one could ever forget 1998. That was the year that was so strong everybody began buying every type of stock, good or bad, just before the recent market debacle—which came to light in 1999 and 2000 just when it should have!

The 1940s were the only decade that did not produce a substantial bull market in the eighth year. The year 1948 was not a bad time to buy stocks, just not a phenomenal one. There was a large rally off the March lows of that year. The March low of the Dow Jones Industrial Average was 165, serving as the base for a rally up to 195 for an 18 percent gain during the year (the Dow closed for the year at about 177).

In using these eight year patterns it appears one should buy about the eighth week of the eight year. Doing so worked wonders in 1928, 1938, 1948, 1958, and 1968. Had you waited until the eighth week of 1978 you would have made your purchase one week from the ultimate low point for the year, while in 1988 and 1998 the low came just a few weeks earlier, in January.

The study of this eighth year pattern should certainly focus our attention on early buy points in the years ending with eight. Accordingly, a wise investor should pay particular attention to 2008, 2018, and yes, we can even forecast out to 2028—when I expect the market to have significant upside performance.

Table 2.1 presents the results of buying in March of each of the years ending in an eight starting in 1878 and continuing through 1998. The exit is on the close of the last trading day in December. While this is not the ideal buy point every year, I believe it does illustrate the important consideration of looking for an early buy point to be long stocks in this subset of years.

I am using Robert J. Shiller's data to reflect the market based on the

Table 2.1   March Buys from 1878 to 1998

Year	March Price	December Price	% Gain
1878	3.24	3.45	6.0
1888	5.08	5.24	16.0
1898	4.65	5.26	21.0
1908	6.87	9.03	21.0
1918	7.28	7.90	9.0
1928	18.25	24.80	26.0
1938	10.31	12.69	23.0
1948	14.30	15.10	7.0
1958	42.11	53.49	27.0
1968	89.09	106.50	19.0
1978	88.82	96.11	8.0
1988	265.70	276.50	4.0
1998	1,023.70	1,190.00	16.0
Average Gain			15.6

Data Source: Robert J. Shiller (http://aida.econ.yale.edu/shiller/data.htm).

S&P Composite Stock Price Index starting in 1871. These monthly readings can be seen on his web site (http://aida.econ.yale.edu/shiller/data.htm).

This is an impressive table of stock market performance, particularly when one considers how far back in time it goes. It illustrates that the decennial pattern has twists and turns to it along the way that an investor should be able to take advantage of.

As I see it, one looks for a low point late in the seven year, and attempts to hold on until late in the ninth year. Table 2.2 shows the same entry with an exit in September.

What we have here is a very important time when stock prices have rallied on a repetitive basis. While I do not have the monthly numbers for 1858–1859 and 1868–1869, you can detect those results from even a cursory glance at the long-term charts shown earlier (Figures 1.1 to 1.5). Those results, taking us back almost 150 years, are very similar to what we see from the hard tabulations presented in Tables 2.1 and 2.2.

Table 2.2   Exit in September of the Nine Year, 1879–1999

Year	September Price	% Gain
1879	4.22	33.0
1889	5.50	8.6
1899	6.37	36.0
1909	10.19	48.0
1919	9.01	23.0
1929	31.30	71.0
1939	12.77	23.0
1949	15.49	9.8
1959	57.05	35.0
1969	94.51	6.0
1979	108.60	22.2
1989	347.30	30.7
1999	1,318.70	22.4
Average Gain		28.3

Data Source: Robert J. Shiller (http://aida.econ.yale.edu/shiller/data.htm).

The data is pretty clear, regardless of how you slice or massage it; but some years are better than others. And on that point, years ending in a three have usually been unkind to investors or have at least presented us with lackadaisical markets. This has not been as true recently as in the past; nonetheless, I feel obliged to point it out to you for your further understanding of future market activity.

3

THE AMAZING OCTOBER EFFECT

*October. This is one of the peculiarly dangerous months
to speculate in stocks. The others are, July, January,
September, April, November, May, March, June,
December, August and February.*
                    —Mark Twain, *Pudd'nhead Wilson*

What Mark Twain did not know was that his in-jest saying actually nailed when most stock markets bottom. Figure 3.1, courtesy of Genesis Financial Data Service, shows along its lower edge the seasonal pattern of stock prices as measured by the Dow Jones Industrial Average from 1970 forward. The small repeated chart is an interesting one in that it averages all of the months during this time. (Earlier we averaged the years, and now we're focusing on the months.) In this fashion the chart creates a seasonal pattern of how stocks have traded in the past. The overall trend is removed from the data so one sees the fluctuations on a month-to-month basis. We are quickly able to notice that there is a distinct tendency of stocks to rally or decline at certain points within the year.

As Figure 3.2 shows, the majority of major stock market buying points in the past 30 years have begun in October. This has led to a market rally that has extended, on average, into the April–May time frame. Then the market is most likely to stagnate or go flat, or even decline. In some cases stock prices simply stall, or there might be a substantial down move into the next October lows. This is an extremely powerful configuration the market has exhibited time after time, year after year. There is just no argument about this. This is the way stock prices have traded for at least the

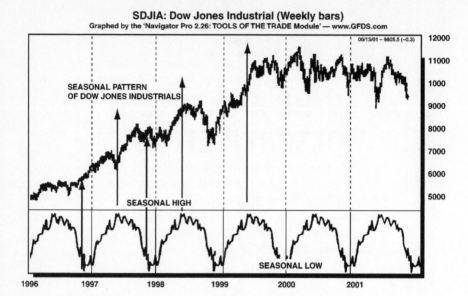

Figure 3.1 Seasonal Pattern of Dow Jones Industrials

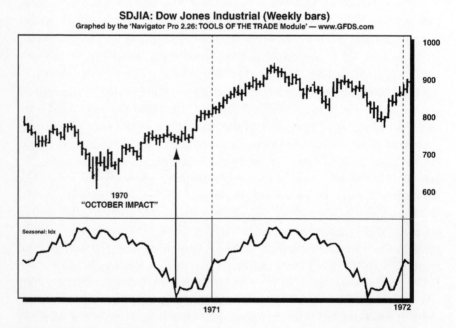

Figure 3.2 October Effect

past 30 years. The question is, of course, will stocks continue to trade in this fashion?

Again, I don't think that the future necessarily will unfold precisely as did the past. Yet it is human nature, as well as most instructive, to look at the past to see how strong this influence might be. In other words, if the influence exists in data before the 1970 time, and is shown there strongly, it would suggest, to me at least, that there is something to this October effect: that in actuality investors are given a timing tool. And this tool is of a precise nature.

Yale Hirsch also did work along this line to see what month's markets were most likely to establish bottom points. His work covered the markets from 1949 to 1975. What he did was simply determine how many important turning points occurred during the individual months of the year. In those 26 years Yale calculated there were 65 market bottoms. The month that recorded the fewest market bottoms and subsequent turnarounds, or rallies, was April. The month that had the largest number of market turnarounds to the upside was October, with 10 out of the 65 market bottoms occurring in this month. The next most frequent month for stocks to turn back to the upside was June.

Yale concluded, "October was the bear killer. Every major postwar bear market (1946, 1957, 1960, 1962, 1966, and 1974) ended here except 1970." I would add to this that while stocks did bottom in the summer of 1970, they rallied up and went sideways, seemingly going nowhere, until October of that year when prices took off on a Carl Lewis sprint to new highs. So while October did not end the decline coming into the 1970 low, it did serve as the trigger mechanism for an important buy point. In typical October fashion we saw yet one more time a springboard or incubator for a gargantuan stock market rally.

There is another study Yale performed we should pay attention to. In this one Yale recorded what the Standard & Poor's index did 30, 60, and 90 days after each month. Those results are shown in Table 3.1. Please keep in mind this study was done on data from 1949 to 1975; therefore, anything after 1975 is out-of-sample data. In other words, again we're interested in seeing how things work out in the future based on what we know from the past.

The gist of all this is that October is ranked first in performance for the 30-, 60-, or 90-days-later calculation. In fact, if we go out six months after October we find an average gain of 7.2 percent. The next closest, or best

Table 3.1 What the Market Did in All One, Two, Three, and Six-Month Periods (26-Year Record, 1949–1975)

			Average Percent Change Between Any Month And					
	30 days Later		60 days Later		90 days Later		6 months Later	
		Rank		Rank		Rank		Rank
January	0.3%	9	1.3%	6	2.4%	5	1.8%	10
February	1.0	5	2.1	4	1.7	6	2.2	8
March	1.1	4	0.8	8	0.7	10	1.8	10
April	−0.3	11	−1.0	12	−0.3	12	1.1	12
May	−0.8	12	−0.1	11	0.4	11	2.2	8
June	0.8	8	1.2	7	1.4	8	4.4	6
July	0.4	8	0.6	8	1.0	9	5.3	3
August	0.2	10	0.8	10	1.8	7	5.3	3
September	0.5	7	1.8	5	2.8	4	6.3	2
October	1.2	2	2.4	2	4.2	1	7.2	1
November	1.2	2	3.0	1	3.6	2	5.0	5
December	1.8	1	2.3	3	3.4	3	2.9	7
	0.6%		1.2%		1.8%		3.7%	
	Average 30-day change		Average 60-day change		Average 90-day change		Average 6-month change	

Based on average monthly prices of Standard & Poor's Composite Index. Reprinted from Yale Hirsch, *Don't Sell Stocks on Monday.*

month for buying, would have been September with an average gain six months later of 6.3 percent. The worst month for a six-month hold would have been April, which showed a net gain of 1.1 percent six months after the theoretical buy point. March and January were not much better, with both also showing a 1.6 percent gain.

On average, the gain of any given month, six months later, has been 3.7 percent. So essentially this means that October has just about doubled the average monthly gain of the market from 1949 to 1975. I decided to test this idea out into the period after 1975 to see what the results would have been. Table 3.2 gives us an additional insight as well as confidence in this overall technique. I assumed buying the Dow Jones Industrial Average on the last day in October and exiting on the last trading day of April.

Table 3.2 Numbers after Hirsch Study

Year	Oct/April % Gain	April/Oct % Gain
1976	−4	−3
1977	+2	−11
1978	+8	−5
1979	0	−4
1980	+8	+13
1981	0	−14
1982	+23	+16
1983	−5.5	0
1984	+4	+3
1985	+29	+9
1986	+21	+5
1987	+2	−13
1988	+13	+5
1989	+.05	−.5
1990	+18	−8
1991	+9	−6
1992	+3	−4
1993	0	+10
1994	+10.5	+6
1995	+15	+10
1996	+16	+8
1997	+21	+6
1998	+25	−5
1999	0	−.5
2000	−2	+2.2
	Average gain 9.05 percent	Average gain 1.1 percent

This strategy, basically that which Yale had outlined in his work, averaged 9.05 percent per year. You should keep in mind that this was not a 12-month hold but a six-month hold. An investor who limits activity to just six months does as well as a person who is fully invested, fully exposed to risk, for a perpetual hold strategy.

The other side of this equation would be to buy the Dow Jones Industrial Average on the last day of April and exit on the last trading day of October. The earlier work showed that April was the worst time to initiate a six-month hold and it certainly did not fare well from 1975 forward. Despite an overall substantial uptrend in stocks, such a strategy would have barely netted an investor 1.1 percent per year—precisely the same average gain shown in the prior 26-year study!

Does it make a difference when you time your buys and sells in the stock market? Oh yes, you bet. In fact, you can and should bet on it. The data clearly shows there is a time to sow and a time to reap. When it comes to long-term investment strategy, decision making, and timing your entry, one should keep in mind above all the importance of buying in October—and looking for off-ramps in April.

The wise investor who sought to buy stocks in October and exit in April made nine times more during the past 25 years than the investor who decided to buy in April and exit in October. I certainly do not want to buck those odds; I want them on my side, working for me, not against me. And while it is true that the market the may not roll out exactly like that in the future, that is how it played out in the last 51 years—a trend I'm unwilling to buck. This is such an outrageous difference that it cannot be explained as a statistical anomaly.

Of greater importance is that these are out-of-sample results based on earlier research that reflected this same bias. In other words, prior studies could have been used by an investor. This is not Monday morning quarterbacking. Table 3.2 shows what took place after the original Hirsch study.

REASON FOR THE OCTOBER EFFECT

As always, when one looks at stock market data and finds a significant bias one wonders why it is there. Is there a reason for this to occur?

I believe there is a very strong reason why stocks do bottom in the October time frame. It is primarily due to a combination of two influences. First, corporations announce their quarterly earnings, which tend to be somewhat dismal this time of year. In short, they get the bad news out of the way and the market digests this usually with an October slide; the bad news brings sellers to the marketplace. This in turn causes the market to become oversold. The market always goes from one extreme, of too many buyers, to the other extreme, of too many sellers. Bad news causes one of these extremes, too many sellers.

Then, however, comes the good news! The Federal Reserve in its infinite wisdom starts to either decrease interest rates or increase the money supply in anticipation of Christmas sales. This is a huge dose of economic stimulation. Such strong medicine impacts investors and is reflected in their emotions and buying activities. One of the strongest influences of stock prices is what the bond market does. When bond prices rally and interest rates are going lower, stocks just flat-out rally. That's all there is to it!

It was summed up best by Hank Williams Jr. in his song, "A Country Boy Can Survive." The lyrics go: "Interest is up, stock markets down, you only get mugged when you go downtown." Listen to that; you really don't need to go to the Harvard Business School to understand economics—it's all in this song! When interest rates are high, stock markets plummet and there is social unrest. When interest rates are low, stock markets rally, people can go out and buy things like homes and cars and they can invest in the future—thus they're happy. During these time periods we find social advances as well as peace. It is truly amazing what prosperity can do for people.

It really gets down to this: When the Fed stimulates the economy stock prices rally. The Fed has a history and reason for doing this during the October time period.

I believe showing you the seasonal tendencies in the bond market can best drive home this point. Figure 3.3 uses the Genesis seasonal index reflecting the trading pattern of the Treasury bond market from 1977 through the summer of 2001.

As you can see, bonds have usually rallied (that means interest rates have gone lower) from about the 20th of October until Christmas week. Naturally, this does not happen every year, but it is what has happened most often. It's just like the old advice: "The race may not go to the strongest and swiftest, but, young man, that is how you bet them." This has been a distinct and predictable occurrence that gives way to the all-important stock market rally at this time of the year.

Besides the thesis that stocks rally when interest rates decline, one could add additional timing significance to investment decisions made in October by investigating what bond prices have been doing. In other words, if bond prices have bottomed and/or firmed up during October (the Federal Reserve is taking positive action) then one could be even more bullish or use this as confirmation to enter into the stock market.

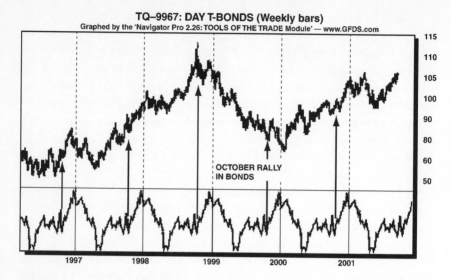

Figure 3.3   October Rally in Bonds

One look at the bond market seasonal pattern and we can see it is no wonder stocks have had such trouble in the first part of the year. The seasonal tendency shows that starting in April, the bond market has been down, usually for the first four months of the year. There is rhyme and reason as to why stocks do what they do. I would like to point out there is a variable lag effect between what the bond market does and what the stock market does. Usually bonds need to rally for a while, say a month or so, before this bullish consideration pulls up stocks.

By the same token, stock market highs do not occur precisely when the bond market reaches its peak but sometime thereafter. By and large, the lead time for this warning from the bond market of potential stock market highs has been anywhere from six weeks to six months. That's the bad news—there's no precise time when stocks will crack because interest rates have started to increase. But I can tell you that every single bear market I have lived and traded through since the 1960s has been preceded by higher interest rates and by a decline in the bond market.

To a large extent, as bonds go so goes the stock market. History is clear on one point: Bonds have most often rallied in October. It is no wonder, then, that the best buying opportunities in the stock market have come at this time.

PUTTING IT ALL TOGETHER

Stop and think for a moment about what we have learned so far: On a long-term basis the majority of important buying opportunities have come in years ending in a two or a three. We can combine the four-year phenomenon with this to load the odds even more in our favor. Hence, we know the ideal buy points would be in years ending in a two that coincide with the four-year cyclical buy point. In the past these years have included 1932 and 1942, both of which were phenomenal once-in-a-lifetime buying opportunities.

The next opportunity came in 1952 when another up move began with a pullback into the first part of 1953. What began then was a straight-up market for the rest of 1953, 1954, and 1955! By the time 1962 rolled around you would think investors would have woken up to this double punch combination of the four-year phenomenon and the decennial pattern. Unfortunately few had. But 1962 acted as the another springboard for one more straight-up market to the record-shattering 1966 high that put the Dow Jones Industrial Average over 1,000. What a beautiful ride that was!

The year 1972 was not a particularly optimal time to buy stocks; but then again *it was not in synch with the four-year pattern*, which had called for a low point in 1970 and in 1974. We had to wait until 1982 for the next ideal buy. That combination seemingly had a tremendous influence on prices, as the ultimate bull market began running almost straight up from 1982 all the way to 1999. Historians now tell us that this was the greatest bull market ever. They didn't tell you to be a buyer at that time, though. Yet the historical record was very clear, as 1982 offered our double punch for a knockout of the bears.

Again, that was why I wrote *How to Prosper in the Coming Good Years*. It was for that reason I went so far out on a limb and risked my entire reputation.

Now that we have seen how 2002 played out, and we note this fits with our four-year phenomenon, certainly the bells of bullishness should be clanging.

Finally, we can bring in the October effect knowing that the majority of bear markets have ended in October. Of importance is that the end of a bear market means a bull market has begun at that time. Thus, I think it is safe to assume that 2002 presented investors with a wonderful opportunity to buy stocks.

When I began this book in the summer of 2001 I thought it would be safe to make another logical conclusion about the future. It was that between then and October 2002 stock market prices would go into a trading range with a downward bias. Would there be a significant bear market? I didn't really know, but there was a little expectation for a substantial move to the upside—until of course we come into our triple whammy buy zone of October 2002, with the four-year phenomenon in a year ending with a two. The historical record of the past suggests there would be some type of significant sell-off between 2001 and our buy point. That would not be out of character, but it was not mandatory that it take place. My study of the past affirms—above all—that our double whammy combination is a prelude to great bull markets. Sometimes these have been set up by significant declines and sometimes not.

WHAT TO DO NEXT

An investor faces several challenges at this point, knowing what we now know. The first, naturally, is to get ready for the next buy point . . . and know what stocks to buy.

Let's not forget that these forecasting techniques tell us we should have a significant market rally in 2005 and another in 2006. That seems to be a pretty good combination, suggesting to me that we will have a great up move in 2005 and 2006. That time represents the next best potential for a major buying opportunity after the one that occurred in 2002.

In either event, knowing this in advance, you should begin looking for stocks to put on your shopping list. The rest of this book will be devoted to selection techniques as well as investment strategies that can be optimized at these superb long-term buying points. Yes, these techniques can be used at other points, but it strikes me as folly to use techniques at what is not an optimal time. Ultimately, I see speculators to be like gambling casinos. Casinos build all those gargantuan hotels, golf courses, and the like simply because they have a small percentage advantage in a game that ranges from less than two percentage points all the way up to five percentage points. With that slight advantage they rake in the dough.

They play their game in an optimal fashion. They make money in the old-fashioned way: They find an advantage in the game and never give you a break (a free room perhaps, but never an advantage over them in their game of choice).

Isn't that what we should do? I sure think so. There's no need to trade every day or even every year. A long-term investor seeks the times with the greatest advantage in his or her favor. As a pilot friend once told me, "It is far better to be on the ground wishing you were in the air than to be in the air wishing you were on the ground."

4

HOW TO KNOW FOR SURE
THE BOTTOM IS HERE

Taurum per cernua prehende.
(Take the bull by the horns.)

We've been able to isolate the times we expect to see the next major stock market lows, that of 2002–2003 as well as the 2005 (decennial pattern five year) and 2006 (four-year phenomenon) buy points. Let's also not forget the potential for a buy point somewhere in the latter part of 2007, the general time when we expect the last up leg in our decennial pattern to kick in, taking us up to the negative first nine and second zero year of this century.

While we clearly have the vision of those potential lows, that will not be enough information to give us the conviction at the time to rush in and buy. I think it will be helpful for us to study market buying points of the past to better understand what to expect and what to be looking for as these potential buy opportunities unfold.

HOW TO TELL WHEN STOCKS ARE UNDERVALUED

There are several indicators I have used and found to be extremely valuable in calling major market bottoms. While there are several ways of looking at what forms a market bottom, one would be the fundamental scenario. There's a great deal of significance to what the yield is on the

Dow Jones Industrial Average. The yield is the amount of cash return investors get from companies in the form of dividends.

In the past, stock market highs typically developed with the yield of the Dow Jones Industrial Average somewhere under 3 percent. That was an extremely good rule until the 1980s and 1990s, when, for whatever reason, stocks continued churning ahead despite the very low yield in the Dow. The yield is a measure of value or quality. Not paying dividends is usually (not always) a sign of a lackluster or unprofitable company.

Major market bottoms in the Dow Jones Industrial Average have been seen when the yield on the Dow was over 6 percent. In light of the fact that a 3 percent or lower yield no longer seems to stop stock market activity to the upside (now undervaluation seems to be more in the 1 percent to 2 percent area) it might suggest to us that the 6 percent yield factor will become an even more rare occurrence than in the recent past, or may not be seen at all.

The 6 percent yield has called, without a doubt, the best major buying opportunities of the past 100 and some years. That is a long-term track record that I don't want to neglect. Nonetheless I am concerned that we may not see such a high yield at the next market low. There have been lows without such a high yield. An absolute fixed rule of investments is that anytime the yield on the Dow Jones Industrial Average exceeds 6 percent one should mortgage the house, scrape up all the possible cash one can acquire, and buy stocks. They may not go up the next day or the next week but there is a gargantuan bull market ahead whenever stocks have had such a high yield. This has hardly ever occurred but the few instances have always led to huge stock market rallies.

The spread between competing yields of stock and bonds is probably the best way to look at these value numbers. Stocks always compete against another investment. So if stocks yield 6 percent but bonds yield 12 percent, clearly stocks are overvalued despite a high yield. *In the markets all things are relative.*

It makes sense to me that if we can double the yield in the Dow from a prior market high then we are in an area that we can call relative value.

Suppose the current yield on the Dow Jones Industrial Average has been 3 percent at the market top. If we were to double that we would get a 6 percent yield, at which point one would look for a market bottom based on value. That has been the general relationship of high yields to low yields in the past. A yield below 3 percent seemed to cause market highs; over 6 percent market lows.

On July 31, 2001, the yield on the Dow Jones Industrial Average was 1.69. Doubling that would be a yield of 3.3 percent. This ought to be the general area where we would next see a market undervaluation point occur. A yield somewhere in the area of 3.5 and 4.0 percent yield would most likely signal the next market bottom area. This would indeed be the highest yield for the past 20 years! The Dow had not been at such a valuation level since 1982. Accordingly, I suspected that if we again got this type of high-yield performance by the Dow it would attract long-term investors. After all, bank accounts currently are yielding about that, yet offer no opportunity for upside appreciation.

HOW TO FOLLOW THE FEDERAL RESERVE SYSTEM

The Federal Reserve Board is as concerned about stock prices as you are. Whether the chairman of the Fed has been Arthur Burns, Paul Volcker, or Alan Greenspan, they have all expressed great concern about higher or lower levels of stock prices. Students of Burns have shown me the models he had developed and surely used while at the Fed.

After all, the stock market has always been the most immediate measure of confidence, and confidence is the currency of every banking system.

It appears as though they have a valuation for stock prices that they have used over the years to help them determine monetary policy. The Fed measure is arrived at by determining the ratio of the S&P 500 to its fair value—that is, the 12-month forward consensus of expected operating earnings per share divided by the 10-year Treasury bond yield minus 100. This is readily available on a web site published by Ed Yardeni (just do a web search for Yardeni or Ed Yardeni). While Yardeni himself has been a bit extreme in his bearishness at times, and in particular regarding the Y2K supposed crisis, he was also one of the few bulls at the 2002 low. The index has done a wonderful job of telling us, and the Feds, when stock prices are too high or too low.

Figure 4.1, showing the index as of September 2001, is pretty simple to interpret. When the index is above 20, historically speaking, stock prices have been overvalued and declines of some magnitude have taken place.

When the index is under −10, stocks have been in a long-term purchase area.

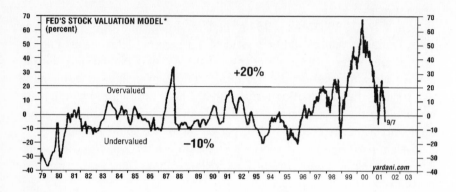

Figure 4.1   Federal Reserve's Stock Valuation Model

Ratio of S&P 500 Index to its Fair-Value (52-week forward consensus expected S&P 500 operating earnings per share divided by the 10-year U.S. Treasury bond yield) minus 100. *Source:* Thomson Financial.

The index topped out at over 65 in 1999, and in 2001 and in 2002 was in the neutral zone. The most logical reading to next appear should be one of undervalued. That is because the market goes from undervalued to overvalued and back to undervalued. Since we were in the overvalued zone we know that the markets are heading for an undervalued zone in the not too distant future.

Accordingly, if you see this index got below the –10 reading in 2003, you will know a low in stock prices should be at hand. At that time investors will be helped by the power of the Federal Reserve system; the Fed will see this reading as a strong indication that stock prices are low and they need to help buoy market activity.

This also drives home the importance of stock market earnings, and illustrates rather graphically how they are the key ingredient to real market success.

Keep in mind that money always has choices; it can go into a conservative and safe investment, such as a bank or savings account earning a fixed rate of return, but in doing so it cannot accomplish any advancement through capital appreciation. When money chooses this option it suggests money is afraid of the future. Yet if money can get a comparable return in a safe haven and still have the potential for upside investment it's a pretty simple choice of where money will go. It will go where it can get the best of both worlds—a comparable yield or return in conjunction with a potential for growth and appreciation.

Money always follows the basic law of human motivation, which is that self-interest prevails, and given a choice of the best of both worlds, smart-money investors, in fact people of all nations and races, will make that most logical choice.

Now feast your eyes on this same chart as it appeared in 2002, as Figure 4.2. Lo and behold, shortly before stocks bottomed, the index had moved into the buy zone I had predicted in 2001.

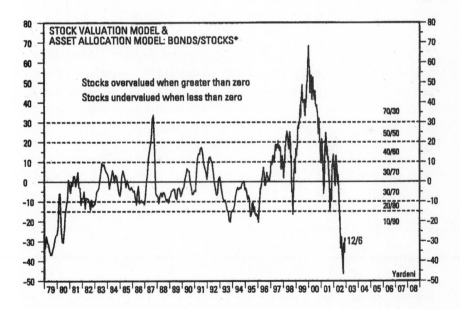

Figure 4.2   Stock Valuation Model and Asset Allocation Model—Bonds/Stocks
Ratio of S&P 500 index to its fair value (12-month forward consensus expected operating earnings per share divided by the ten-year U.S. Treasury bond yield) minus 100. Monthly through March 1994, weekly after.
Source: Thomson Financial.

ADDING FUEL TO THE FIRE

Money, cold hard-earned cash, is the mother's milk of market rallies. It is the singular stimulant and ultimate fuel for all upside activity. When the gas tank is full, this car can go forever. The fuel largely comes from:

I *Stock Mutual Funds*—These guys get their money from folks just like you and me, folks from all walks of life, rich and poor, wealthy and superwealthy. In recent years pension fund dollars have also topped off the tank.

I *Private Investors*—Private investors may either pony up their own money exclusively or borrow from their brokerage firms on margin to seek even more bang for their buck. To that extent their ability to borrow these funds is the potential for fuel. When they are all loaned up, the tank is empty; when they have borrowing power the prospect of a brighter moon looms on the night's horizon.

To a large extent, the tremendous influx of mutual fund money has buoyed stock prices in the past decade. One could truly say that cash fuels the engines of higher stock market prices. This cash may come in from individual investors or may come in from mutual funds or even from governments and financial institutions. Currently mutual funds are the big player in the game, at times accounting for almost 60 percent of the volume in the marketplace. This percentage has been consistent both before and after the crash of 1999; thus it is of great value to see how much cash these funds have on hand.

When mutual funds are sitting on a great deal of cash it means they can buy—they can add gasoline or fuel to the fire of upside activity. When they have very little cash on hand—that is, on a relative basis—it's very difficult for prices to go higher because the gas tank is empty.

From 1982 forward, when the funds were sitting on more than 8 percent cash, markets had a distinct tendency to rally. The best buying opportunities from 1982 forward came when the funds' cash position was over 10 percent. Other high readings occurred at the 1985, 1986, 1987, and 1990 buy points.

It would be nice then, wouldn't it, to see the funds in a cash position of somewhere over 10 percent. It may not even have to get that high. On a three- or four-year look-back basis, if the fund position were to get over 8 percent it would indicate the largest cash position of the past four years, which should be bullish toward a market rally. The higher the cash position grows, the more bullish it will be, as there is more fuel for higher prices.

Mutual funds' cash on hand is such a significant index that it is of extreme importance to follow it. It can be found in *Barron's* or *Investor's Business Daily*, and you do not have to look at it every single day of the week. This information is released once a month, which is adequate because it is such a long-term index. It is fundamental to the structure and causation of stock market up-and-down movements, so it certainly should be on your list of important stock market indicators.

A "FUELISH" THING TO DO

Brokers often encourage their customers to borrow money to purchase stocks. The amount an investor can borrow is a function of how much money is in the account and what the loan ratio on those funds is. Frankly, I think it is unwise to borrow to trade or invest. Of course, when you are right it's to your advantage, and if you can beat the pipers—that is, earn more than the broker's interest rates—you'll make more than if you had not borrowed.

But when you are wrong you are doubly injured: you have lost money that was not yours. I'm content to earn what I earn without increasing liabilities, but then I don't like debt. Been there, done that; it's not all it's cracked up to be.

Figure 4.3 shows 37 years of the S&P 500 index with margin debt (the money investors borrowed) overlapped on the same chart. Two things are at work here: As stock prices go up, customers' equity increases, enabling them to borrow more. And as prices go higher investors are prone to borrow more, and more, and more. This borrowing is the fuel to the fire, as you can see. Exponential increases in debt are harbingers of rallies.

Now let's look at the ability of the private investor to buy more stocks due to his or her ability to borrow money. Figure 4.4 depicts the annualized 12-month rate of change of stock market margin credit extended by the New York Stock Exchange (NYSE) member firms. When borrowings have been increasing by about 40 percent more than a year earlier this "source of fuel" has been about used up. Virtually every major market high from 1970 forward has been tipped to the astute investor by such a

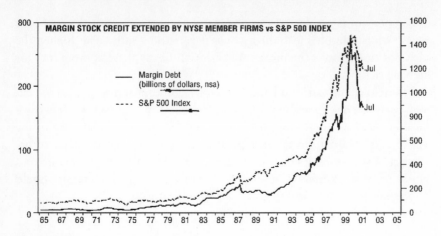

Figure 4.3   37 Years of S&P 500 Index with Margin Debt

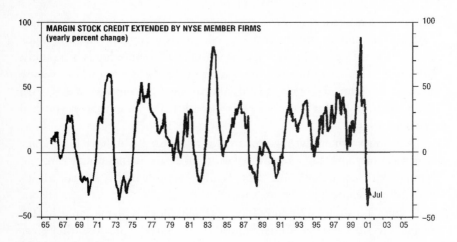

Figure 4.4   Margin Stock Credit Extended by New York Stock Exchange Member Firms

reading. Granted, this does not pinpoint the exact high; it's just a message that the party is ending, the last dance has begun.

The reverse is equally true: When there has been a substantial decrease in credit (ie., private investors have *not* been borrowing money to buy stocks) there exists the *potential* for them to begin buying. It is for that reason that most market lows since the late 1960s have occurred about the same time the 12-month rate of change of credit was –20 percent or more.

Again, this is not a pinpoint, precise tool. But its record of suggesting when a major market bottom is close at hand is, indeed, excellent. You can judge for yourself, as this index was clearly indicating that a market low was due in the fall of 2001. Additionally, as of the end of 2002 the index was still under the zero level, telling us to expect higher prices.

I would love to see this index at –20 percent or close to the other buy points I have listed in this book. That would be wonderful confirmation.

INVESTOR SENTIMENT IS THE SECRET TO INVESTMENT SURVIVAL

If there is any one secret to investment survival it would be to understand that to a very large degree swings in the stock market are in response to investors' emotions. While on a long-term basis stocks may be going higher, the intermediate-term highs and lows along that route are caused by investors getting extremely bullish or extremely bearish. I can think of no better short- to intermediate-term indicator than that offered by a study of what the majority of investors are doing. Interestingly enough, this can be mutual funds or individual investors. Perhaps best of all, or perhaps we should say worst of all, is what the investment advisers themselves are saying.

It is ironic, but absolutely true, that when the majority of investment advisers become excessively bullish stocks decline.

By the same token, when the majority of investor advisers become excessively bearish stock markets rally.

It is of great importance to understand this because at virtually every stock market low you'll find investment advisers, newspapers, brokers, and the like to be negative on stocks. They will be reticent and reluctant to buy. They will tell you not to do what you have to do. This flies in the face of everything you have learned your entire life. We have always, outside of the markets, looked to the experts to tell us what to do.

So when the experts are not telling us to buy we don't buy. The stock market, though, is a totally different world than the one we live in every day. Here the world is turned upside down; what seems good is bad, and what looks bad is very, very good.

There is a reason for this. Investors, be they advisers, mutual funds, or simply individual folks like you and me, are primarily influenced by the appearance of trends. The more the market advances the more bullish we become. The more a market declines the more bearish we become. This seems to be an immutable law of psychology. It is the way the human mind works. It is almost as though investors are acting as judge and jury seeking more information and more information in order to come to a conclusion. When all investors reach the same conclusion, the game is over.

If there is a reason for this, it is simply that there is no more fuel from these investors to keep the engines of growth churning. The market runs out of mutual fund fuel or public investor fuel.

As my good friend Tom DeMark said, "Markets don't top because sellers come into the marketplace. Markets top because there are simply no more buyers." That's it! See? When there is nobody left to buy there's no more money to drive prices higher. When all of the investors or investment advisers are already bullish, there simply isn't much more buying to come into the marketplace. Stocks have no choice but to decline. There are numerous ways of looking at the psychology of the marketplace. I would like to quickly review these for you.

The public is perhaps best reflected in an indicator of market activity called "odd lot short sales." This index simply shows the percentage of transactions of fewer than 100 stocks that are being sold short. The thinking is that an order for less than 100 shares is most likely an order from the public. That's because the investor placing such an order does not have enough money to buy 100 shares where there's usually a big commission break. This should reflect public money (i.e., people without much money)—in any event, the uninformed investor. We have records of odd lot short sales dating all the way back to the 1920s. Looking at more recent data in Figure 4.5, we see they have a very good record of being heavy short sellers right at market lows.

As an example, notice the odd lot short sales just before October 2000 buy point. What we see is at that time 14 percent of the odd lotters' total activity, longs and shorts, were on the short side. In other words, they became aggressive and heavy short sellers right at the market low, exactly when they should have become buyers!

By the time January 2001 rolled around the short selling odd lotters had dipped down to about 4.5 percent, right at the market top! A study of the recent past suggests we need to see odd lot short sales get above 10 percent. That's the time we should expect an important market low to be at hand.

It has not been in vogue by market analysts and technicians to monitor odd lot activity for quite some time now. I am of a different opinion. Per-

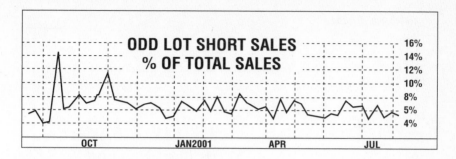

Figure 4.5 Odd Lot Short Sales

haps that's because I have so ingrained in my work the study of these people—I have seen them do the wrong thing for so long. They do exactly the opposite of what we want to do. Plus, I don't think markets always bottom the exact same way. What I'm looking for is a preponderance of evidence that the public is excessively bearish. That's what you want to look for in the spring of 2003 as well as the other buy points we anticipate out into the future. If I notice just one of the sentiment indicators to be in the correct zone, that's enough for me to confirm that a projected buying opportunity is indeed at hand.

ILL-ADVISED INVESTMENT ADVISERS

There are several ways of monitoring what the investment advisers are doing, and all need to be paid attention to, as these people have such a splendid record of doing the wrong thing at the wrong time. Frequently they are worse than the public.

Investors Intelligence, an advisory service, monitors the number of newsletters and investment advisers that are bullish or bearish. (See Figure 4.6.) Their records show that when 55 percent or more of these advisers become bullish the market is most likely to go down. Investors Intelligence breaks its indicators down into a study of advisers who are bullish and advisers who are bearish.

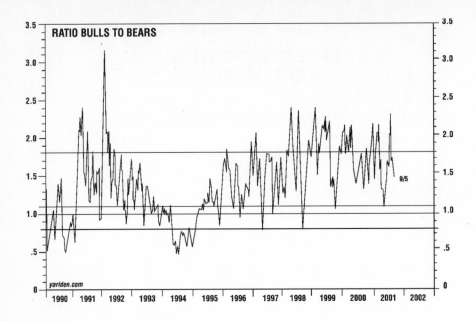

Figure 4.6   Ratio of Bulls to Bears
Source: Investors Intelligence.

When 35 percent or fewer of these advisers are bullish, the majority are then bearish, and markets are most likely to go up.

Striking evidence of this comes from the market high seen in January 2001. At that time over 60 percent of investment advisers were bullish in mid-February just before the Dow Jones Industrial Average took a ravaging decline to the downside. Unfortunately, it has been some time since investment advisers were overly bearish. I suspect, however, as stock market prices continue to slide into our projected buy zone or just go flat, we will once again see the Investors Intelligence measure of investment advisers dip below 35 percent bullish.

This indicator can be viewed in *Investor's Business Daily*; it usually appears in the lower left-hand corner of the page showing the charts of market activity. This currently would be the last page of the first section of the newspaper. This value is reported on a weekly basis for your further understanding of market activity.

We can use this same approach for measuring individual stock activity as well. In Chapter 9 I will show you my sentiment index, which is a measure of investor attitude toward individual issues as opposed to the entire stock market. Again you'll see the same thing: When the index is showing excessive investment advisory bullishness, an individual stock is most likely to go down. When the majority of investment advisers' attitudes are reflected in excessive pessimism, an individual stock goes up the vast majority of the time. Not all will every time, but it's a better bet and a darn near ideal bet if the stock you are buying is fundamentally sound. There's lots more coming on selection in just a few moments.

HOW TO USE THE BOND MARKET TO PREDICT THE STOCK MARKET

A long-term study of the relationship between the bond market—that is, interest rates—and the stock market forces the serious student to reach one conclusion: Higher interest rates—that is, lower bond prices—are bearish for stocks. There is a very good reason for this: When interest rates are increased, corporations must pay off their friendly bankers before they can pay off shareholders. At times such as this, dividends may be cut and earnings drop for several reasons.

If bankers have to be paid a greater amount than when interest rates were low, then there's no money left over for research and development or primary expansion of the business. As if that is not enough, the problem is magnified by the fact the customers of the corporation are in this same predicament. They now have less disposable income; thus they do what is only natural—they cut back on orders. Sales of products and services decline because the net effect of higher interest rates is to take money out of productive circulation in the form of interest payments.

Of course, this has a snowballing effect. Fear then sets in, causing more cutbacks and leading investors to cash out of the market.

When a company can't pay dividends or expand through research and development and more production, the stock of a company loses its upside momentum; earnings decline and shortly thereafter so does the price of the stock in question.

The other side of this coin is that when interest rates are lowered companies have more money to advance the cause of their business; credit is easier so they can finance further expansions to reach the goals they have on their agendas. An increase in money supply is about the same as a decrease in interest rates. Both are positive phenomena to the economy and the ability of a company to grow and have more prosperity.

Well, that's the theory, and it is clearly borne out by a study of interest rates from the mid-1850s all the way into the year 2001. The problem is putting this theory into practical application. There are some very sophisticated mathematical models that seek to exploit this relationship between stocks and bonds by developing buy and sell signals. For the most part the math is not only complex but also difficult to run, and some of the data sources are not easy for the average investor to come by. Some analysts are more concerned about municipal bonds or Treasury bills or 10-year notes and the like, others about the electric utility index on the Philadelphia Stock Exchange! Really!

An additional problem presents itself in that sometimes bonds bottom shortly before the stock market bottoms while at other times the lead time may be months instead of weeks. Some analysts, notably Gil Haller (*The Haller Theory*, 1968), one of the most genuine people I have ever met in this business, looked at the amount of change in Treasury bills on a percentage basis to predict stock market rallies. His thesis was that a full percentage point decrease in interest rates was enough to turn a down stock market into an up market.

I can simplify much of this approach to forecasting stock bottoms in a mechanical fashion by using an index created by Welles Wilder and Gresham Northcott. The index was first presented to investors in 1978 in a book by Wilder entitled *New Concepts in Technical Trading*. There are many good indicators in this book. One of my favorites is known as the volatility stop or volatility system.

This is a trend-following mechanism that works by taking the range (each day's high minus the low) for the past seven days and then multiplying this average range by a factor usually in the 2.0 to 3.0 value. This is an amount of volatility, which is then subtracted from the highest closing price in the uptrend.

What is created is a filter band above and below the current price. Should the stock price close below this point the assumption is the trend is down.

When prices have been below this volatility filter and close above the volatility filter the trend is then considered to be up. This can be used on daily or weekly charts.

MARKET TIMING USING BONDS TO BUY AND SELL STOCKS

It is my observation that this volatility index, when applied to the bond market, gives us an indication that interest rates have bottomed. My assumption is that if the trend in interest rates has bottomed—that is, the bond market is beginning to rally—then stocks should shortly follow thereafter.

Figure 4.7 shows the bond market on a weekly basis with the volatility stop. Our trading rule would be to look for a point to buy stocks when the weekly close of the bond market is above the volatility stop. This should take place during a time stocks have been declining or a bear market has been in existence. We are using the trend of bonds to buy stocks. *When the weekly close of bonds is greater than the volatility stop we'll mark off a point to buy stocks.*

The next few figures show the results of this system from 1982 forward

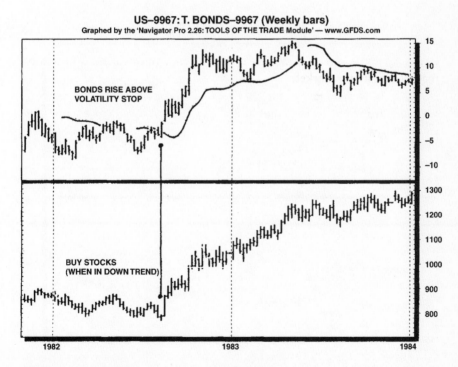

Figure 4.7 Volatility Stop, Bonds 1982–1983

so you can see for yourself. Please understand it is used only for *entering* the market—this is not a sell short indicator.

On Friday, August 13, 1982, bonds closed above the volatility stop, suggesting an up move might begin in stock prices. The question was, would it really begin? Well, the rest is history. As you can see that was the same week stocks made the bottom that began the gargantuan bull market that has now been billed as the largest in the history of mankind.

As shown in Figure 4.8, the bear began to walk on Wall Street in 1984 as stock prices declined into August of that year. Investors were worried. Was a new bear market beginning? Was this the start of a continuing market slide?

Those questions were argued from the boardrooms and barrooms of Wall Street to the bedrooms of Main Street. The argument could have been settled by simply looking at what the bond market had been doing as the stock market continued declining. In the summer of 1984 bonds began to rally; then in the week ending August 3 bonds closed above the volatility

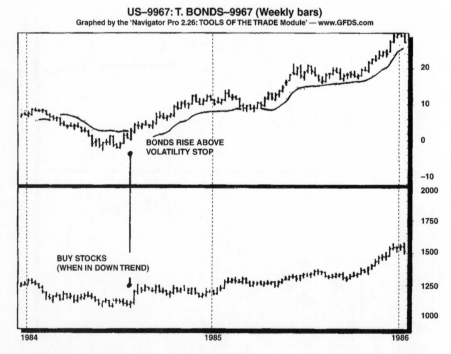

Figure 4.8   Volatility Stop, Bonds 1984–1985

stop, which was one week before the ultimate low in the bear market! Our volatility stop rule heralded the resumption of a major bull market. Not bad for such a simple index. Would it work next time around?

By late 1986 it was apparent stocks could be in trouble (see Figure 4.9). Although they had not moved substantially to the downside, they had stagnated, leading investors to question what was going on. Was this a time to buy or a time to sell?

Turning our attention to the bond market instead of newspaper headlines, we would have noticed that in the week ending December 5, 1986, bonds once more closed above the volatility stop, suggesting it was time to buy—a time for optimism, not pessimism. That buy signal gave birth to an immediate and substantial up move taking stocks to a new all-time high in 1987.

Then, along came the crash of that year complete with the largest one-day market decline investors had ever seen in any market in any country.

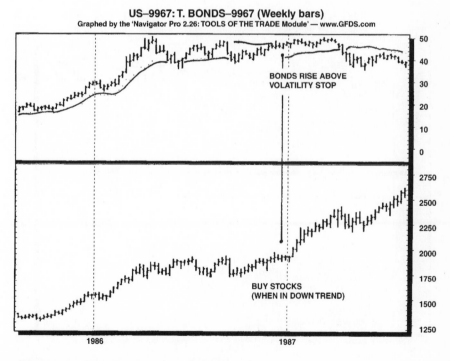

Figure 4.9   Volatility Stop, Bonds 1986–1987

(See Figure 4.10.) It was a true panic; brokerage firms went bust, investors were wiped out, and mutual funds that had been worth $3 billion were suddenly worth $2 billion—all in the blink of an eye. Blood had been spilled on Wall Street in that fateful October, and investors panicked. Not knowing what to do they sold and sold more, causing massive liquidation and breaks in the prices of individual stocks. It was a far-reaching disaster.

During the week of the crash I was on a safari in Africa. By the time the news of the 600-point down day reached where I was staying, the Mount Kenya Safari Club, the panic had reached proportions we had only read about in the historic crash of 1929. Within hours, over two-thirds of the people staying at this luxurious resort packed their bags, changed their flight schedules, and were headed home for damage control. Women were spotted crying in the dining room, with their ashen-faced men. It was not a pretty sight, but then losing money never is.

Had those investors simply taken the time to study the bond market they would have seen something bullish beyond belief: Black Friday—that

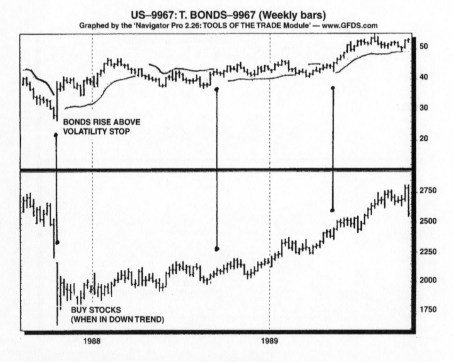

Figure 4.10   Volatility Stop, Bonds 1988–1989

is, Friday October 23, 1987—saw the bond market once more close above the volatility stop. The crash was over almost as quickly as it began. The crash of 1987 consolidated, and the market regained its control and breath as a new bull market began. What actually began the new bull market will be argued for years, but one thing is certain: Our bond market buy signal was there at the precise low! Investors knowing this could have bought all the stocks they wanted and made a killing while others were being killed.

Things went well for stockholders until 1990, which is just about the time we would expect the market decline based on our decennial pattern. After all, what are zero years for? They are for declines. That's nice to know, but it's even nicer to know when to buy. Using our bond market buy signal for the stock market, an investor would have noticed bonds had been below the volatility stop until the week ending November 9, 1990, a scant four weeks after the stock market had bottomed and very close to the low itself (see Figure 4.11). Stock prices had not yet begun to advance. Investors

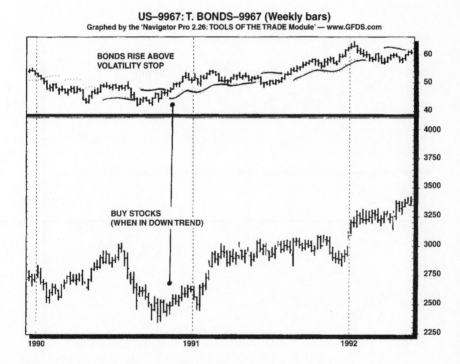

Figure 4.11   Volatility Stop, Bonds 1990–1992

who purchased at these levels were quickly rewarded as yet one more up leg came into play. Starting to see how all this works?

All was well and good until 1994, when stocks began to stagnate, oscillating back and forth, up and down—seemingly directionless (see Figure 4.12). No longer was it a one-way path to instant stock market wealth. The bear was again on the prowl. Investors were frightened and wondering whether another crash like that of 1987 was ahead of them. Would this miserable "go noplace" market get healthy, or would it hit the skids?

On December 23, 1994, stocks had rallied for a brief three weeks, but there had been many similar rallies such as this in the past that had only led to further market declines. This time something was different, though: The weekly closing price of Treasury bonds had exceeded the volatility stop. A buy signal was given and investors were told interest rates would most likely go lower and stock prices higher.

It is interesting to note that this particular buy signal, which came right at the start of a year ending with a five, produced the most rapid up move-

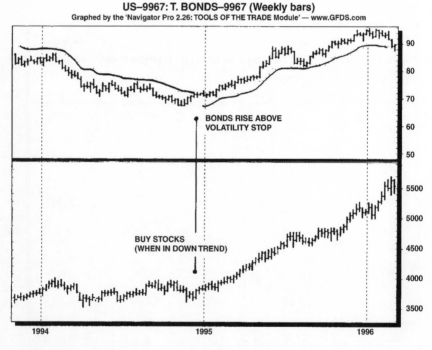

Figure 4.12 Volatility Stop, Bonds 1993–1996

ment of the 1982–1999 bull market. It was clearly evidenced as a bull market buy point by our bond market trend change signal.

The "tech wreck" that came to the marketplace during the middle of 2000 saw value cut beyond anyone's expectation. Stocks that been selling for over $100 a share went to $80, then $50, then $30, and then below anybody's wildest predictions, dropping to $10 and in some instances $5 a share. While 1987 was a big crash, it was over within one month. Companies came back for better and brighter days. But that was not the case in the crash of 2000. Not only did the stocks not come back, but in my judgment (as you'll read when I discuss individual stocks) most of these never will come back, or at least not for the next 6 to 12 years.

As you may have noticed, from 1982 all the way to 2001, each and every significant buy point was preceded or indicated by our simple bond market/volatility stop penetration. Let me remind you there's no magic to this approach. The precise value of the volatility stop is not what makes this work. What makes this work is the fact that we have an objective way of determining when the bond market has most likely hit bottom. That's important because bottoms in the bond market mean you are at, or very near, bottoms in the stock market.

The relationship between stocks and bonds is a fundamental consideration to the marketplace. It is not some mumbo-jumbo technical line drawn from point to point, some unproven charting technique or junk science approach to forecasting the markets. We are talking about what moves the economy: interest rates. They move the economy. Charts don't move the economy; conditions move the economy, and conditions move the stock market. I know of no simple and better way of measuring this than the volatility index approach.

The final chart, Figure 4.13, shows the results of this same simple indicator during the tough sledding of 1999–2002. There were only two buy signals, the first on August 24, 2001, a scant four weeks from the year's low. In 2002 the buy signal came in the week ending June 21, five weeks before the low of the year.

LOOKING AHEAD

There will be bear markets and bull markets in the coming good years. It is our objective to determine when the tide has turned, when the buy points are at hand, when the slides are over. We now have two excellent

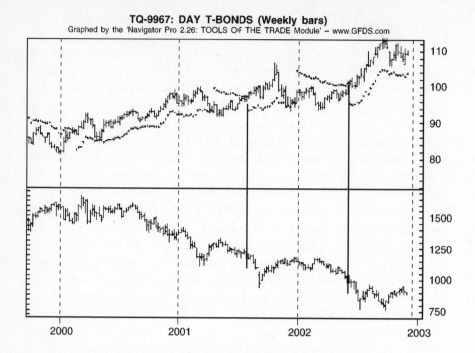

Figure 4.13   Volatility Stop, Bonds 1999–2002

fundamental indicators to help us. One is the value or yield on the Dow Jones Industrial Average, the other the trend direction of interest rates and the bond market. We can couple this with investor sentiment, using odd lot short sales and investment advisers along with mutual fund activity for our major timing tools.

If I had to choose just one of these tools it would be the bond market because it is precise, readily available, and simple to follow. Seldom in history have bonds rallied without an ensuing up leg in stock prices.

There is an old adage on Wall Street that says, "The trend is your friend," and that is true, "at least until the end." The problem is identifying when the beginning and end occur. Now you know the conditions seen at the end of most bear market slides. Accordingly, it is my wish that you go forth and prosper, keeping your eyes peeled to these invaluable indicators. I expect they will call buy points in 2003 and 2005 and speak rather loudly once more when the four-year phenomenon gives us yet another buying opportunity in 2006. Indeed, whenever stocks have been in a bear market, pay attention to the bond market. A significant change in direction there is the key you are looking for.

GOING BUGGY OVER GOLD: BREAKING THE GOLDEN RULE

The golden rule of life is not the same as the golden rule of the market-place. For years investors, advisers, and financial authors have proclaimed a relationship between gold and the stock market. One of my favorite questions to ask at trading seminars is simply this: "If the stock market crashes, what will happen to the price of gold?"

The investor response is unanimous. "Gold will rally!" the crowd roars back.

"Oh," I ask, "is that so? But what about the crash of 2000? What did gold do then?" I see furtive glances around the room. I've got them trapped. Chart books open, mouths drop, bodies squirm . . . then the realization sets in. Gold declined in the crash of 2000. (See Figure 4.14.)

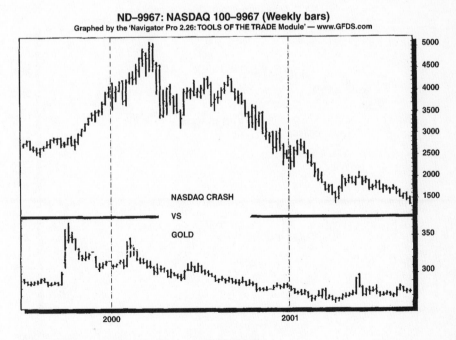

Figure 4.14   Nasdaq Crash versus Gold, 2000

I then ask about the crash of 1987. What did gold do then? As you can see from Figure 4.15, gold went sideways during the crash of 1987. It is with irony that I point out that the largest rally in gold of that year came after the crash was over, in December 1987, long after the bottom had been put in.

The next step is to take the seminar attendees back to the crash of 1929, so they can see for themselves what happened back then. They expect to see a substantial rally in the price of gold. But they don't see it, because it didn't happen. Gold has never had a substantial rally during a stock market crash!

Isn't that interesting? It's been an old wives' tale, a tall tale at that, this supposed relationship between gold and the stock market.

If you are a gold bug, be a gold bug for the right reason. Depressions don't make gold go higher. There are only two considerations that cause gold to rally, in my book: The first is inflation; the second is what the commercial users and producers of gold are doing. Seldom has a major market

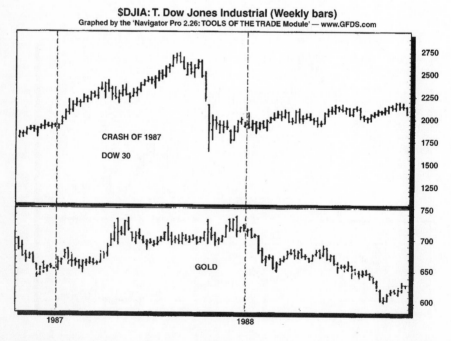

Figure 4.15   Crash of 1987 versus Gold

rally in gold taken place without the commercial interests first becoming heavy buyers of this precious metal.

Even a cursory glance at charts or study of history shows that gold rallies the most during times of inflation, not times of depression. Stock market crashes are depressing not only to investors but also to the entire economy. Even to gold bugs. Indeed, there's a time to sow and a time to reap. When it comes to the gold market, it, too, has its natural cycle, which is a product of commercial demand and inflationary pressures. That's what to look for here. Now you know my golden rule for the gold market. It is not that he who has the gold gets to rule; it is that he who has the smarts gets to buy gold at the right time.

Figure 4.16 shows the tremendous impact the commercials have on this market. What you are seeing here is an index that measures the percentage of net longs the commercials have positioned themselves with. This is an actual measure of what they're doing with their money. Most

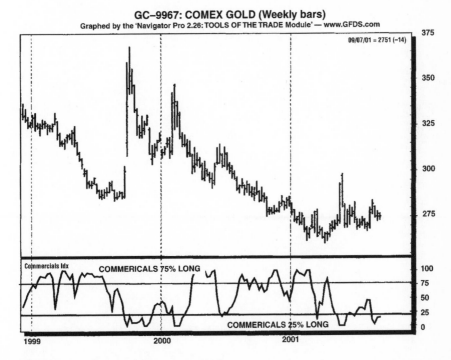

Figure 4.16 Commercials versus Gold

often, when they become aggressively long—that is, they have a high reading of net long positions—the gold market rallies. Note their large selling in the fall of 1999 and subsequent crash, or their buying in early 2001 and later a rally.

By the same token, when they are aggressively short or have not been doing much buying (that's indicated by low reading in the index), gold has shown a distinct propensity to decline.

If the gold bug camp would pay attention to what the commercials are doing they themselves would have a much better idea of when to get in and out of this market. It is unfathomable for me that anyone would think there could ever be a significant market rally in gold without the commercials first assuming heavy long positions. So, if gold is your thing, follow the commercials; don't follow the pipe dreams or any emotional reactions of would-be market gurus. All they have invested are postage stamps and words, while the commercials, who are in the business of using or producing the precious metal, have plunked down millions of dollars.

5

THE NEXT MOVE UP: WHY IT WILL BE SO SPECTACULAR

It is better to learn to say no than to learn Latin.

Stock markets do many different things for many different reasons, but behind every market move there's a common element: human emotions, which are motivated by greed and fear.

I think it is important for us to look at the current investment climate to see whether it can help us ascertain how the future might unfold. If we can get even a glimpse, be it ever so small, of what will next drive stock prices up, and down, we will have in part beaten the game—in part made ourselves smarter than and placed ourselves ahead of the rest of the investment crowd.

I have given this a good deal of thought, studied markets from the past, and talked with fund managers and investment experts whom I have come to know over the years. From that I have synthesized what I think is an important overall concept for us to consider regarding the next stock market up move.

What I believe will happen as the next bull market begins to roar to the upside is that frustrated, pent-up investors (people who lost money or those who wish they had made money in the last bull market) will hop aboard like we have never seen before.

I do not believe that at any time in history of mankind there have been more people more interested in future stock prices than now. Being an investor is now not only popular but easy. In the old days it seemed to take a certain acumen to become an investor. You had to know something—be part of an informed minority. Brokerage firms were, to some extent, out of the reach of the average person. That is no longer true, as now you can trade from anyplace at any time. What was once privy to the few now has two television channels.

It is almost as though we went from an industrial revolution through a technological revolution to an investor revolution. The revolutionaries of yesteryear have become investors. Everyday conversations now focus on the stock market, with the stock exchanges sponsoring sporting events, and brokerage firms sponsoring golf tournaments and such. Wall Street has taken on the popularity and depth of McDonald's!

There is a tidal wave of investor money on the sidelines just waiting for an excuse or reason to purchase stocks, and nothing makes investors more impatient than a market that rallies when they are not long. At some critical point they just can't stand it any longer. The up move in prices will confirm to them to start a bull market and the floodgates of cash will open. Stocks will be purchased, in record numbers. It's going to be awesome!

Couple this, if you will, with the basic nature of mankind, which is to have more, to be greedy, to enjoy money, and to want to work for it. The public has seen the incredible amounts of money to be made in the stock market, and they will not be held in check. The huge Nasdaq rally and its many success stories, even though many turned into failures, whetted the public's appetite for stocks. No longer is the public ignorant of the market-place. While it is true they may currently be on the sidelines, they're ready to suit up and come to play.

This may get the point across to you a little better: When I began trading stocks, the *Wall Street Journal* was very much a niche newspaper with precious few lay subscribers and even fewer newsstand sales. Its customers were brokers and investors. Compare that with now, when the *Wall Street Journal* is available in grocery stores and news racks throughout the world. The *Journal* has gone from about 20 pages a day up to almost 100 pages to fulfill investors' needs for more market information.

On top of all this we have an investor base that now has money. We have not seen a major economic recession for almost 30 years; hence, capital has been building. Whether it is in retirement funds, bank accounts, or mutual funds, there is now money in circulation, more than ever before in the history of mankind. And that's all it takes to start the bull market stampede—money!

We know history is the past, and the past never repeats itself precisely. Yet the public mind believes the future can and will become almost identical to the past. So they look back at the price activity of a few select stocks and see that a meager investment of $10,000 or so could have been turned into millions. Their interest is piqued. They want some of that action, and they will come into the next bull market.

Unfortunately, I don't think they will be there at the start of the bull market. That doesn't make sense. The public never buys at the market bottom; they get in midway, then become heavy buyers of the top of a market. That's fine—because I'm going to show you how to use that to your advantage.

LESSONS OF THE PAST

The first lesson from the past it appears that the public has learned is that stock market investing can create massive sums of wealth, the type of wealth people dream about—and spouses nag about not having. This creates a huge potential demand for stock, gallons and gallons of fuel to be added to the fire.

While I do not expect these investors to buy even close to the low point of the marketplace, they will come into the game at some point. Rising stock prices create a feeding frenzy with both the public and pros. So, let's ask ourselves, when they come in, what game will they want to play?

The answer to this can also be learned from a study of the past. Some of these people are experienced. They have been around the track a time or two, and are as aware of the run-up of the market as they are the run-down of the market. The public mentality, regardless of how you measure it or how you slice it, has changed from being infatuated with high-tech, new economy stocks to being downright frightened of the same issues.

They have seen fortunes lost as high-tech ideas collapsed and washed ashore onto the desert island of profits. Originally that desert island idea was simply to find some great high-tech stocks to own that, even if you were on the desert island, by the time you were rescued would have made a fortune. There is still an assumption this can take place, though investors of the future, I believe, will be more judicious and less willing to take high risks.

At some point this will change. Close to the top of the next bull market we will again see massive public buying that will create a frothy wave of price activity. Keep that in mind. It will happen. But as the market begins its rally once the public sees the trend has resumed to the upside, that the game is back in town, when they first enter they will be buying quality and value as opposed to getting carried away with speculative issues. Let me be clear about this: Later in the game they will turn their attention to spec stocks, shortly before things collapse. Highfliers of the day will prevail again, but not as the bull market starts to become known to the public.

When? Well here's what I wrote in the first draft of this book in 2001, just as presented to thousands of traders and investors:

If I'm correct in this view, and I certainly think I am (check it out for yourself, however), it means the stocks we want to buy at the October 2002 low are quality stocks that will be attractive and feel safe, warm, cuddly, and fuzzy to the public investor who will buy enough of the stocks to drive the prices higher, thus enhancing our investment returns. We want to get in early on the stocks that all this public money will pour into. It's as simple as that.

Well, 2002 has come and gone. I'll let you judge the prediction.

I believe the funds will turn their attention from stories and rumors of a new economy to shopping around looking for good growth companies. This means companies that have earnings, companies that pay dividends, companies that do have bricks and mortar, machinery, equipment, employees, and real physical assets as opposed to computers acting as store. Oh, sure, there will be high-tech stocks that do well, but by and large the bulk of investor gains will come from the tried-and-true, proven, so-called old economy stocks.

Companies with earnings, growth, and dividends are the ones that will prosper. These are the ones the public will seek out. And there will be more than just the public lifting these prices ever upward. Mutual funds themselves have learned the same lesson.

The only way a mutual fund can stay in business is to have some type of positive performance for its shareholders. No positive performance, no shareholders—that's the basic math of mutual funds. Managers of these mutual funds are just as susceptible to the path of least resistance as the rest of us, and when they see that a particular type of investment is succeeding over another they go in that direction. It's human nature.

Let's look at how these guys do. A study I did of the top 25 growth and income funds, for the six months ending in August 2001, showed their performance was downright miserable. Only five of the top 25 funds showed profits for 2001.

Yet, if we look at the top 25 value funds for the same time, all but one of them showed profits for their shareholders. What a difference! Value prevailed; growth did not. Finding profits in growth has become a most difficult thing to do.

How badly the funds have been doing reflects on how much they will change their investment strategies. In July 2001, the largest reporting service on mutual funds, Lipper Inc., revealed to investors that 4,120 of the 5,208 United States stock funds it followed lost money!

That is an incredible figure. It means almost 80 percent of the mutual funds were in the red for the year. They will have to change their strategy. It is almost as though these funds have no choice but to invest in quality at this particular time in history. They, too, just like the public, will go into a state of rapture later in the bull market and resume their bad habit of buying rumors and future growth. But right now the big word on Wall Street is value as expressed by earnings dividends and companies that do real business.

The slide of 2002 was not handled any better by the funds. In December, so-called growth funds were down 23.6 percent and technology funds were down 39.5 percent while value funds were tagged for only a 15.8 percent loss. Overall mutual funds were down 25.6 percent while the S&P 500 was down only 21.2 percent! Again the funds on average did not better the market. You can do better, and that's exactly what you will learn in this book.

You are getting off easy reading a book about learning this lesson. Contrast that with the folks who began the IPO and New Era Fund in August 1999. Life for this fund started with a bang: In its first three months of doing business it was up 89 percent on the some $10 million under management the founders had attracted to their concept. Their concept? Buy new offerings and be aggressive purchasers in high-tech stocks. One of their supposed strengths was that they were based in San Francisco, high atop skyscrapers where they could carefully monitor the money machinations of Silicon Valley.

This fund was supposedly a new breed of cat. To show how honest and open they were, all of their purchases were listed on a web site. They even went so far as to mount a Web camera in their trading room to offer investors a personal look into precisely what their traders were doing. You did not have to be an investor in the fund to watch and/or debate the positions with managers and traders of the firm.

Some good it did. In August 2001 they had to shut the operation down, as they had lost half of the funds under management, thus being forced to close shop and return what was left of the funds.

That is exactly why in 2003 and for several years to come the big word on Wall Street will be value as expressed by earnings dividends and other ratios I will teach you. Our profits will come from companies that do real business.

This trend will be with us for some time, leading me to believe that as the first buyers of the new bull market we want to buy what is going to attract these people. It sure seems clear to me they will want to buy what we are going to own, at least if we follow the advice in this book. Our goal is to own good long-term growth stocks that fit value molds in the various forms discussed in this book.

The headaches and heartbreaks of the bursting Nasdaq bubble will be with investors for the next three to five years. After that time they will most likely have forgotten the importance of consistency; greed and jealousy will get them again as they see rapid rises in the issues where they have no positions. That's exactly what causes investors to throw good judgment to the winds as hormonal greed glands overrule thoughtful logic. Seeing someone making money when you're not, seeing someone outperform you, is the worst kind of pressure, the kind of pressure that causes emotion to overtake logic.

We are in an economic environment with cash-heavy investors from all ages and all walks of life. Yes, the 1999–2002 crash was real, and lots of people lost lots of money. But it was paper money—paper profits. There were also people who took their profits, left the game early, and have cash. The decline "cost" investors $6 trillion, but that money did not all evaporate. Much of it is still there, awaiting the next bull market. That money is burning a hole in their pockets; they have a hangover effect from speculative Nasdaq profits they did not participate in or did not nail down. That's a dynamic combination to produce upside activity in value stocks.

But there's more to the story. We're not talking about just the United States anymore. The U.S. stock market has become the premier investment vehicle for people from all over the world. While America may have lost some of the dominance in terms of world influence, it has not in terms of economic clout. Sure, we've had our Enrons and Adelphias, but our stock market is less tarnished and more regulated than any other exchange on this little planet. Couple that with this simple fact: The best investment opportunities—ideas—are still developed here, in the good old U.S. of A., and you know there is a huge future ahead of us. In 2002 the corporate accounting scandals may have tarnished our image but capitalism is still more transparent in the United States than almost anywhere else in the world. Money may have temporarily fled the view of the Department of Justice but it will be back.

The Yankee dollar is the yardstick by which all other currencies are measured. More great business ideas have come out of this country than all the others combined. We are terribly unique in that we are one of the few countries of the world where business is not conducted by bribery. Yes, we have bad eggs in the United States, but they are the exception, not the rule. Things are done here for the most part aboveboard, which gives investors the opportunity to see what is really happening.

Notice how the U.S. dollar, as shown in Figure 5.1 has fared over the

Figure 5.1 U.S. Dollar 1986–2002

past 17 years. It was in a steep downtrend from 1986 into 1995, yet the American economy steamrolled upward. Currently it has had about a 50 percent correction of the 1995–2001 bull market. The Yankee dollar still reigns supreme. I see no reason that will change.

I have lived in Europe and the Middle East, and have conducted business in Asia, and I assure you that how we do business is not exactly how business is carried on there. Corporate raiders and critics don't have a clue as to how well-off we are here in America.

Who does have a clue are large foreign investors. That means anytime there is a significant bull market within United States equity markets, their money leaves home and comes to our shores, into our marketplace, driving prices even higher. The European banking system loves American stocks. I believe there are several reasons for this; one was cited earlier, and another is that the growth of corporate America is based more on business and the profit motive than stodgy European family ties.

In Asia, the financial community is replete with multitiered business relationships and more business angles than Minnesota Fats ever saw on a pool table. Investors feel more comfortable knowing that there is more truth to the American marketplace than their own.

At any given time, someplace in the world there's a government that is being toppled, an overthrow of a regime, an economic system or approach ruining a country. That has not been the case in the United States, nor do investors think it is even a remote possibility. This concept is intrinsic to understanding why foreign investors like our stock market so much. It is because we represent stability, growth, and fair, aboveboard corporate relationships.

So, in addition to private and mutual funds to spur the next bull market ever upward I believe we will also have a rush of funds from all over the world to our shores to buy stocks in the finest United States corporations. If this is to be the case, as I suspect it will, we can pretty well predict the type of stocks they will be buying. They, too, have learned a lesson of chasing high-tech growth and momentum stocks and the like. This time around they will go for what we, hopefully, will have purchased at the next major stock market low.

If you are fortunate enough to get in just slightly ahead of the large funds and foreign money, you should see much greater gains, coming much quicker, than will those who hop aboard the train after it has left the station.

KEY TO UNDERSTANDING INVESTORS

It's not too difficult to figure out what investors will do. They have a very strong habit of looking at the past to figure out what to do in the future. By now they have learned to stay away from the type of stocks that turned into debacles the last time around; hence, technology stocks will not get their vote.

When they look to the past they will focus their attention on the spectacular up moves that numerous stocks have had, stocks such as those featured in the *Worth* magazine editor's choice selections. A good many investors are still in those stocks, and others will put their attention on the stocks in the assumption that what was once high will again go up.

All our lives we've tried to buy things cheaply. Discounts appeal to us—we like to make purchases of things that we think are low-priced, that are worth more. Nowhere is this better evidenced than in the stock market. Investors get carried away with low-priced stocks thinking about spectacular up moves—particularly if a low-priced stock used to be high-priced.

PATTERN FOR DISASTER

Accordingly, I want to show you the pattern for disaster—a simple chart formation I've noticed through the years that has been highly reliable. Frankly, I haven't made money on this pattern, but I've used it to prevent me from losing money, which is equally important. The pattern is one I first noticed in the price of sugar in 1962.

Sugar had one of those spectacular run-ups that started from a long-term base, then turned into a straight-up exponentially rising market. Fortunes were made, happy times were here. It looked impossible for prices to go down.

Which, of course, they had to do! The top was formed with a sharp snap setback in the marketplace, then an almost immediate and startling rally. But the rally didn't take sugar to new high prices. It almost immediately gave way to yet one more wave of selling, which took out the low that the last-ditch rally began from.

In short, sugar had a spectacular and exponential up move, a pullback, then a rally that failed. Sugar continued declining for years, from 1962 until 1973.

In the mid-1960s I saw the same pattern again, this time in the price of one of the all-time high-flying stocks of that era, Syntex. Again there was an exponential rise in price, a pullback, and a last-ditch rally attempt, then a break of what had been the low point prior to the last-ditch rally. It was all over. Syntex didn't come back. Yet investors thought it would. The company was still in the same business, making the same products; yet the price of the stock got so overvalued or out of balance with reality that the high prices investors paid became a thing of the past never to be seen again.

In many instances, with companies such as Hoe & Co. or KleerView or Astrodata in the 1960s, the stocks not only plummeted after the exponential up move pattern occurred, but the companies went out of business! It is almost as though the price can withstand only so much of an exponential move without internally breaking the back of the corporate camel for a long, long time.

Another leading example, one shown here (Figure 5.2), is the price of gold in 1978. Again there is a huge exponential up move, the typical break,

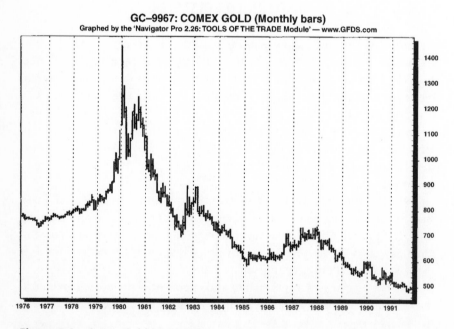

GC–9967: COMEX GOLD (Monthly bars)
Graphed by the 'Navigator Pro 2.26: TOOLS OF THE TRADE Module' — www.GFDS.com

Figure 5.2   Comex Gold 1976–1991

then last-ditch rally. Gold never came back—not in 1980, not in 1982, not in 1987; it just simply couldn't get going again. Check out the all-time high in wheat as well (see Figure 5.3 and 5.4). I am showing numerous examples of this pattern for your study (Figures 5.5 through 5.12).

The all-time "made in America" example of this pattern came with the crash in 1929, which looks strikingly similar to the Nasdaq crash of 1999–2000 (Figure 5.12). Look, there it is again: Those doggone nine and zero years keep popping up—or down I should say.

I believe there is a reason for this pattern of run-up, pullback, and failed rally. It is largely due to the fact many investors hold onto stock from the highest level. At some point later on they give up the ghost on these investments and sell into virtually any rally the stock or commodity might see. In other words, we have a tremendous amount of overhead supply, which acts as a damper to higher stock prices. Rallies are met with huge doses of selling, people taking their licks and getting out of their long positions. Mutual funds also come into play in this scenario. Most of the funds have dumped their stocks by the time prices have come down this far, though, so they may not be responsible for much of the overhead supply.

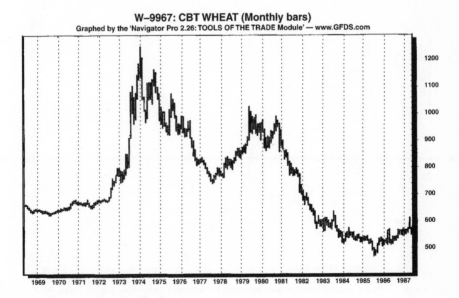

Figure 5.3 Wheat 1969–1987

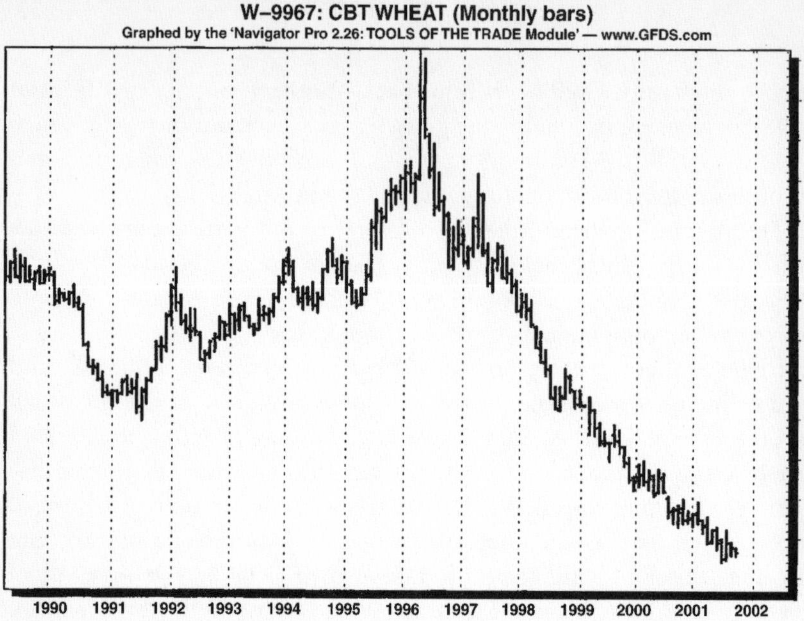

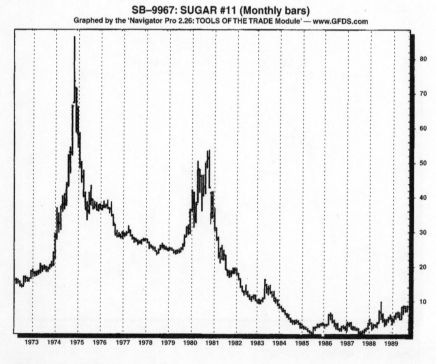

W–9967: CBT WHEAT (Monthly bars)
Graphed by the 'Navigator Pro 2.26: TOOLS OF THE TRADE Module' — www.GFDS.com
900
850
800
750
700
650
600
550
500
450
400
350
300
250
1990
1991
1992
1993
1994
1995
1996
1997
1998
1999
2000
2001
2002

Figure 5.4 Wheat 1990–2002

SB–9967: SUGAR #11 (Monthly bars)
Graphed by the 'Navigator Pro 2.26: TOOLS OF THE TRADE Module' — www.GFDS.com
80
70
60
50
40
30
20
10
1973
1974
1975
1976
1977
1978
1979
1980
1981
1982
1983
1984
1985
1986
1987
1988
1989

Figure 5.5 Sugar 1973–1989

Figure 5.6 Sugar 1979–1994

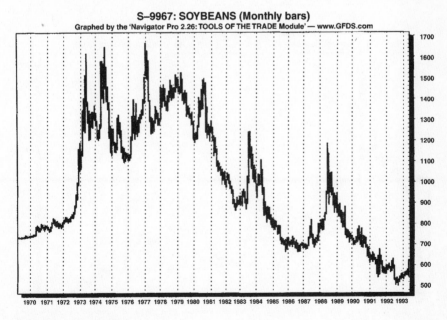

Figure 5.7 Soybeans

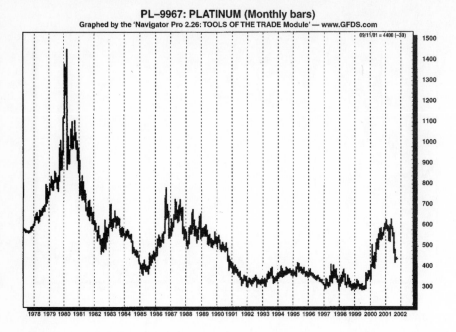

Figure 5.8 Platinum

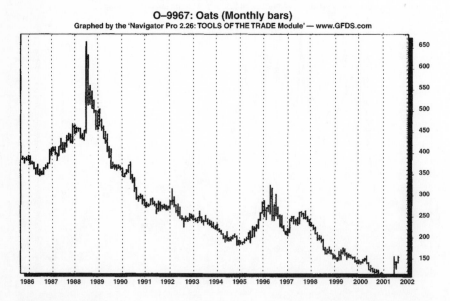

Figure 5.9 Oats

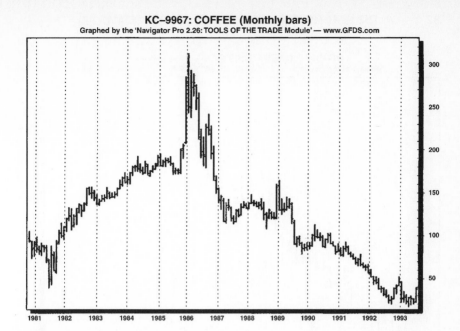

Figure 5.10 Coffee

Figure 5.11 Japanese Yen

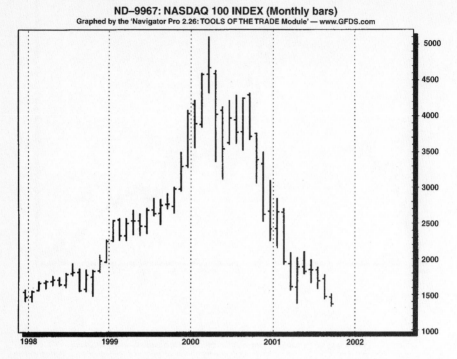

ND–9967: NASDAQ 100 INDEX (Monthly bars)
Graphed by the 'Navigator Pro 2.26: TOOLS OF THE TRADE Module' — www.GFDS.com

Figure 5.12   Nasdaq 100 Index 1998–2001

However, they'll never touch these fallen angels again. The institutional support the stocks once had, which drove them higher, no longer exists. Now the big boys don't want them, as the stocks are an embarrassment to have in their portfolios. Even if you know the prices are low enough to represent value, nobody wants to hold losers or stocks that are now perceived as being turkeys. Once a stock loses institutional support it is very difficult for the public, on their own, to drive prices substantially higher. Those stocks continue to be laggards dwindling ever downward, redefining the law of gravity only in that they fall at a lesser rate than before.

This is an extremely important pattern, one I hope you'll burn into your mind so you won't get burned by buying these falling-dagger types of stocks. Don't get lured into buying by some fast-talking broker who goes on about how high the price once was. That's the past. There's virtually no assurance, or even an indication, that high prices of yesteryear create high prices in the future. In fact, if we look at this argument (prices are low now compared to where they once were, hence they should go back to where they once were), we see it is obviously flawed.

The problem in discussing strictly price activity is that there's no focus on earnings, dividends, growth within the industry, or what the company is doing. We have short-circuited the logical rational process of making sage investment decisions by saying there is apparent value because prices are low relative to where they have been. More fundamental to the situation is that the prices are low for a reason. The back of the camel has been broken, and these exponential markets don't come back for anywhere from 6 to 12 years. It takes that long for one of these stocks to get its act back together, to refresh its bad name, clean up its image, and once more attract institutional support to its side.

A CLUE TO THE FUTURE OF THE NASDAQ

Since the sack attack of the Nasdaq, investors and friends have asked me what I think of this market, which translates to "When will my stocks come back?" I'd prefer not to answer the question, because I know they'd prefer not to know the answer. "The best analogy," I tell them, "may come from looking at what has happened in Japan. Here," I continue, "look at the long-term chart of the Nikkei. Notice how similar it is to the Nasdaq. See how it had that exponential rise in 1989 (notice the decennial nine year pattern there, too). Gee, does that look to you like the Nasdaq?" I ask.

That's about the time their mouths drop open; then they say, "Yeah, the up move looks like the one here, but that was 14 years ago. Are you telling me that's what's going to happen to my stocks?"

"Probably," I say as I try to get away from them, "especially if the companies you have invested in don't have any earnings or the price of the stock is relatively high compared to the company earnings."

That's when they start mumbling about these being growth companies, part of the future, that they will go back where the once were—that these companies won't go out of business.

I shake my head as I give them my last two cents of advice: "Bite the bullet—these sad sacks are not coming back. The Nikkei, gold, and commodities are your model to study."

6

THE PURPOSE OF INVESTING

Skating on thin ice is better than not skating at all.
—John Shanahan

Everyone wants to get rich, to have an ample amount of money whether to spend or to brag about. Making money has become as popular as Perrier water. A generation of BMW-buying yuppies coincided with a bull market that created wealth beyond many people's expectations and wildest dreams.

It came so quickly, though, that most investors have not given much thought to the purpose of their investing. "Girls just want to have fun"; people just want to make money. Exactly how this is to be accomplished is often thought of more as some chance phenomenon—something to do with luck, being in the right place at the right time—than as the product of clear thinking and diligent research.

As far as getting money is concerned, it all begins with your intention to get rich. Without intention there can be no productive long-term gain. However, the path to hell is lined with good intentions. That's why I think purpose demands a great deal of our attention, so that we might bring our intentions to fruition.

If your purpose of investing is to get rich quickly, then a different strategy is needed than that of the person who wants to accumulate wealth over a time period. I would suggest to you that getting rich quickly, which can happen in the stock market, is not as likely and carries with it a much higher degree of risk.

Risk, which is what we are all exposed to as investors, is largely a function of two ingredients we need to examine. The first of these is time, the second selection.

Let's first look at the investment possibilities that exist. There is certainly more to the investment world than the stock market. There are other very good vehicles for investment: bonds, your own business, real estate, and for some investors, gold or precious metals. To this list I would also add art and/or historical artifacts. Each of these has its advantage but only real estate and stocks have consistently performed and provided an investor with ample data to make intelligent decisions.

I happen to collect art of a particular fashion. The problem with it is that not only is beauty in the eye of the beholder, but so is price. Plus, there are no daily or even yearly figures published on what is the value of the items I have collected. I collect because I love what I collect; this has little to do with capital appreciation. It is an extremely difficult market to follow unless you simply follow your heart.

That certainly doesn't sound like a way to make money, does it? Yet it is not unusual to see these rare old items sell for 10 times what one paid for them. Like any investment, some of these items don't go up in value, and some may even go down. The best thing is that there is no holding cost, no painting, mowing, plumbing to fix, tenants to collect from, or printed price fluctuations seen daily. There's just the enjoyment of art . . . pure pleasure.

THE BEST INVESTMENT YOU'LL EVER MAKE

Let's stop and think for a minute about where all this money comes from. How is it investors have cash to plunk down into mutual funds and/or the stock market? It has to come from someplace. Oh, sure, it might come from a retirement plan, but what created the money for the retirement plan? Either the private sector or the government funds all retirement plans. Keep in mind that the government gets much of its money from the private sector through income taxes—taxes on salaries generated by private businesses.

Hopefully, you'll agree with me, based on this scenario, that the creation of wealth throughout the world comes from businesses. You may despise the giant corporations, rail against them as much as you want, but you cannot argue away the bottom line: that productivity and wealth are generated from the corporate sector or entrepreneurs. This could be a mom-and-pop operation or IBM. It doesn't matter—this is where money gets generated. Governments don't generate money; they confiscate it.

Accordingly, the best investment you can ever make is in your own business. Admittedly, some people don't have the desire to have their own business; they would rather work for somebody else than take the risks that go with creating an entity, an enterprise that assumes huge responsibilities and obligations. But the old adage will always hold: Without risk there can be no gain. It is far less risky to take a job than it is to create your business; hence business owners, if they're lucky, are rewarded more than their workers are.

So, if you have some spare change you are seeking to invest, I would first encourage you to seriously consider the creation of a business enterprise as opposed to investing in Wall Street or any other place. With that behind us, I'm now assuming you have created your wealth through your job or career and have that base in order. Typically, people say you should have insurance and real estate as the basis of your investment. I think that is totally incorrect. Holding onto real estate does not generate cash; buying and selling it does. An insurance policy pays off only if you die, and doesn't strike me as a very smart investment scenario.

I believe people have realized this at some cosmic level, which is one reason why so much money poured into the stock market in the late 1990s. Real estate can be an extremely good investment. Typically, people think of real estate as an investment to protect them from inflation. In times of an inflationary economy real estate appreciates and immense fortunes have been made in this fashion.

I believe it is safe to say that real estate is not a better long-term investment than common stocks. This is for two reasons. First of all, usually real estate investment means taking on debt. The debt is a large cost of doing business, so while your friendly real estate agent can show you that prices have appreciated X percent over the prior 20 years, he or she neglects to point out that there was a cost of holding onto these properties. That cost may have been a lot more than just interest rates. The actual amount paid for a house is usually three times the sales price due to interest charges on the debt. What's more, that house had to be painted, mowed, trimmed, insured, and otherwise kept up, and, of course, taxes had to be paid. When you deduct the cost of holding the asset as well as a commission structure of 6 percent to buy and another 6 percent to sell, the numbers don't look nearly as good as on the surface.

Again, that's not to say there isn't money to be made in real estate. Fortunes have been made there. But for the most part, these fortunes were made by investors who understood the marketplace. What I see is that in most instances, these investors had a substantial amount of capital or superior lines of credit. Even these people, however, have run into financial problems. But if you know your area where you live, and have a great sense of the future growth direction, then there surely is money to be made in real estate.

Some of the things I like so much about the stock market are that there is very little cost of doing business, commissions are low, no insurance is needed, I can sell in an instant, and I don't have to worry that my stock will burn down, the plumbing might break, or the tenants won't pay me. It is pretty cut-and-dried, I can monitor my investment from anyplace in the world, thanks to the Internet, as well as a plethora of stock market publications.

This same advantage exists for those who want to invest in precious metals. You don't have to take delivery of gold. You can simply hold onto a certificate of ownership. Yet a study of the very long-term price appreciation of gold shows that it has substantially underperformed not only stocks, but real estate as well as Treasury bonds and Treasury bills. In fact, on a long-term basis gold has not kept up with inflation! Yes, there have been some great rallies in gold, but I'm talking long-term here.

While I am on that subject let's point out that long-term government bonds, while they have beaten Treasury bills for a total return from 1925 to 1999, have barely kept ahead of inflation, especially relative to the stock market.

Had you "bought" inflation in 1925 your total return by the start of the next century would have been an appreciation of 9.2 times your money. That means an item that cost one dollar in 1925 cost about $9.20 in 2000. Had you bought Treasury bills your investment of one dollar would have grown to almost $15. Had you bought long-term government bonds your return would have been much better: $44 on that one dollar invested all those years ago. Had you purchased real estate, on average, one dollar of real estate would have returned approximately $100, a profit more than double the return on long-term government bonds.

However, had you purchased blue-chip stocks your one-dollar investment would have become worth more than $2,000!

You would not have needed great expertise to have purchased quality stocks, and you could have begun with any amount; financing was never required, and you never had to walk into a bank to beg for a loan.

Doesn't this all sound good? If only it were that easy—buy something and hold on to it. The problem that stockbrokers neglect to tell you is that while their total return tables show that $2,000 of profits, that is your return only if you had the wisdom to purchase the blue-chip stocks that survived through all the years. Many of them didn't! So what we have here is a selective process that assumes you bought stocks that were the winners. But that may not have been the case. Most investors, most of the time, do mostly the wrong thing.

FALLACY OF LONG-TERM INVESTING

There's a common myth, when it comes to stock market investing, that all one needs to do is purchase quality stocks and hold onto them for the long pull. That simply is not the case; it is a very misleading position. The only thing we can say for sure about the long run is that in the long run most people die.

Let me point out some specific examples for you. Ford Motor Company has always been a major blue-chip stock, and in recent years it has fared well. However, if you purchased it in the late 1970s, as many did for the $2.60 a share dividend it was paying, you would have received $26,000 a year in income from an investment in 10,000 shares.

By the time 1984 came around, the long-term buy-and-hold strategy wasn't working so well as the dividend was cut to $1.73, reducing your income to $17,300; and of course the price of the stock declined. Things didn't get much better. In 1981 the dividend was cut to 80 cents, so instead of receiving the $26,000 a year revenue on the 10,000-share investment, you were now getting $8,000. The trends persisted. In 1982 the Ford Motor Company paid no dividends at all. An investor who had purchased Ford, a typical blue-chip stock, was left holding the bag. The long-term strategy, as practiced during a 15-year waiting period, had not been successful. Investors were severely burned by the strategy.

Stocks don't always go up—even blue-chip stocks. There's a reason for this. As I see it, long-term investors are the biggest gamblers in the marketplace; they make their bet and stay with it. If they are wrong they can lose it all, as they never change their chips on the table of speculative investments. You bet, there are lots of examples where the strategy has paid off. Those are the ones you hear about, but there are a heck of a lot more instances were the strategy did not pay off, where the long-term buy-and-hold strategy was a failure. Such stories don't make for very good cocktail conversation. Investors are unwilling to discuss these occurrences. That's why you never hear about the negative side of long-term investing in stocks.

Here's a list of blue-chip stocks I'd like you to take a look at. Would you like to have been a long-term holder of this portfolio?

American Express
Avon Products
Disney
RCA
Westinghouse
Polaroid
Honeywell
Howard Johnson

What we have here is an excellent list of profitable corporate giants— but not a good group of stocks to own in the 1972 to 1974 time period when, as a group, they declined in value more than 80 percent!

Yes, you read that correctly. Had you purchased at the wrong time, the 1972–1973 high, you would have seen your investment dollars diminish by over 80 percent as these issues made their lows. Wow, that's pressure to sit through as you wait for the long-term trend to bail you out of your problems! Having second thoughts about the wisdom of the long term, the notion of buy and forget it? Good, you should.

Some lessons are never learned. While the supposedly blue-chip stocks of 1972 and 1973 certainly had their comeuppance, it was nothing compared to what happened in 2000 and 2001. One of the more prestigious financial publications was the very popular *Worth* magazine. Their editors came up with stocks that they identified as "the best representatives of the new economy. . . . The editors chose the companies listed here on the basis of their sound of business plans, high-quality products, solid finances, efficient operations, and capable managers. The companies must also operate in markets with the potential for explosive growth."

The editors of this magazine must have had at least a modicum of market savvy and experience to have landed their editorial positions. I doubt if these writers were fresh off the first train into town. They had some very glowing commentaries about these stocks and the new economy. Here is their list with the prices of their recommendations in August 2000 as well as the prices in August 2001 and at the end of 2002.

	August 2000	August 2001	December 31, 2002
Applied Materials	$ 81	$ 48	$ 11
Broadcom	$ 259	$ 44	$ 16
Cisco Systems	$ 65	$ 20	$ 13
CMGI	$ 37	$ 2	$ 1
eBay	$ 56	$ 61	$ 67
Enron	$ 88	$ 45	$ 0
Millenium Pharmacies	$ 111	$ 31	$ 8
News Corp.	$ 52	$ 37	$ 26
Nokia	$ 41	$ 21	$ 15.5
Oracle	$ 83	$ 18	$ 11
Charles Schwab	$ 38	$ 15	$ 17
Sun Microsystems	$ 122	$ 17	$ 3
Sycamore Networks	$ 154	$ 7	$ 3
WorldCom	$ 35	$ 14	$ 0
Total value	$1,222	$380	$185.5

Now you see how expensive chasing high-flying growth stocks can become. Investors who followed the editors of *Worth* magazine (perhaps it should be dubbed "*Worse* magazine") would have lost almost 85 percent of their money. I don't know what you think, but I suspect it will be years and years before this list of hotshot stocks comes even close to the breakeven point for investors who thought they had such a sure thing. That was a rather expensive subscription, proving my point that market education is either worthless or invaluable; there are few in-betweens.

In the August 2000 issue of *Worth* the editors touted the 31.8 percent year-to-date gain this list had made as well as the 116 percent gain for prior 12 months. That doesn't mean much now. What it does mean, or what we should learn from this experience (other than canceling your subscription to the magazine) is that it is a precarious and dangerous game to play catch the leader. Most often the leader ends up at the rear of the pack, and you become the one who has been caught holding a bag full of busted hopes. It's a simple fact of investment life that once the majority of investors catch on to what the hot stocks have been, the game is just about over.

It is best expressed in this fashion: Once the average Joe investor learns the key to the combination of unlimited stock market wealth, somebody changes the combination!

LEARNING IT ONE MORE TIME

The infamous speculator Jesse Livermore summed it up best when he wrote, "I believe it is a safe bet that the money lost by short-term speculation is small when compared with the gigantic sums lost by so-called investors who have let their investments ride. The intelligent investor will act promptly, thus holding his losses to a minimum."

You may want to think of it in this fashion: Betting on tomorrow is a dicey deal full of risk and chance. Now, imagine making that same bet on a day 20 or 30 years into the future. Can you see the craziness of thinking you can see that far into the future? People are lured into the idea of long-term investing because they don't have to make many decisions, don't have to work at it, and love the idea of a long-term nest egg. Thinking they have some type of long-range plan gives people a cozy, warm feeling—they have their lives all figured out.

A good investment can turn into a long-term investment, which is why each and every investment we make needs to be constantly reevaluated in light of changing circumstances in your life as well as the marketplace.

So, the time frame an investor chooses is equally important to the vehicle he or she chooses to invest in. If you recall, when we looked at the seasonal patterns of the Dow Jones Industrial Average, we saw that it has major ups and downs usually lasting from six months to a year or so. But clearly, there's no straight up path to stock market investing. Never has been, never will be. Thus it seems to me that the purpose of our investing should be to get in at the right time and get out at what is also the right time.

Admittedly, we can never do this in a perfect fashion, but the data is very clear that even partially succeeding at this on an intermediate time frame is much more successful than the long-term "buy and pray" strategy.

If your purpose is to buy stocks for gains of six months to a year or so, I think you'll do far better than short-term traders or long-term holders.

WHAT STOCKS TO INVEST IN

I think it is safe to say we can break down virtually all stock market investment strategies into one of two categories. The first is the one that appears to be the most popular; it consists of buying the hot stocks, the in vogue stocks, the ones people talk about after work and during work and that are bandied about in the news media.

There will always be hot stocks—some group of securities outperforming another group. That's just the way it is. Given some 7,000 stocks, rest assured there will always be some leading the pack, but that doesn't mean they will continue leading the pack. My experience with this group of stocks—let's call them the highfliers—is that they run very hot and very cold. Virtually all highfliers that I have seen over all these years of trading have crumbled at some point. That's a point where I don't want to be, a point where I don't want my money.

What rises rapidly doesn't stay there, so while some investors may get aboard these rapid rises, and have exceptional profits, it's a bit like playing Russian roulette. If there is a bullet in the chamber and you spin it often enough one will come up and you lose. Since it is a safe bet to say that all high flying stocks eventually have their down days, and years, I have chosen to avoid the fads of the day because I know these stocks are in actuality being set up for substantial declines. It is not unusual to see high flyers in bankruptcy . . . to see the flyers declining from $100 a share to $15 a share. That's an absolute circumstance, it is irrefutable, it is the key problem that is part and parcel of buying what's hot. High flying growth stocks are a bullet in the chamber of investing.

It's just like the Bible says, "The first one now, shall later be last". I do not want to take a chance of buying stocks that suddenly slip into last place.

CONSISTENCY HAS ITS REWARDS

I'm more than willing to let the crowd chase the hot issues of the day, making what they call "momentum plays"—hoping there's a greater fool out there to buy what they bought at a high price at yet an even higher price. That is really the heart and soul of their game; they seek whatever is moving, with some juicy provocative story, which usually simply separates investors from their hard-earned cash. There's only one way to get that cash back, which is for the stock to continue its parabolic up move. Although that can happen, when these babies crack they break badly. In one day many stocks have given back 20 to 30 percent of the entire gains they had made for investors. When they break like that, investors become locked into the stock feeling they can't get out because it has declined so much. They have no alternative; what began as an investment is now forced upon them as a long-term hold.

I want a safer bet than that. My bet is on consistency. What we do know for sure about the long term is that value ultimately prevails; it is rewarded. But we also know the long term is ephemeral; the long term is made up of chunks of good times and of bad times; our focus is the good times. That's why our vehicle for investments is that of the more secure and less speculative. We will gladly leave the prospect of substantial gains to other investors. They may get them (I hope they do), but the reality is they probably won't. It is tempting to think of those large gains, but if we look at the performances of the top 25 growth funds, for example, we can see how difficult it is for professional investors, people who manage billions of dollars, to achieve exponential gains in their portfolios.

Keep in mind that these are the people who are right on top of the highfliers. They have the best research in the world at their disposal, it is their business to catch highfliers. Can it be done? It doesn't appear so, not when we see that they don't do a very good job, judging from their published performance records. If they can't do it, how could we possibly expect the average Joe to succeed at this obviously difficult game?

There is a real lesson to learn from the interesting data shown in Table 6.1. What is shown here is a tally of the 25 top-performing growth funds from the market high of October 1990 through mid-August 2001. The largest percent gain was racked up by Smith Barney with a 567 percent increase, while the fund in the 25th place gained a healthy 368 percent. On the surface that sounds most impressive.

But we need to look a little bit further to see just how good this performance was. Had one simply purchased the Dow Jones Industrial Average

Table 6.1 Top 25 Growth Funds, October
1990 through August 15, 2001

Mutual Fund	Percent Gain
Smith Barney A Aggressive	567%
Van Kampen Funds A	554%
Vanguard Funds Prime Cap	516%
AIM Funds Aggressive	499%
Waddell and Reed	492%
Federated Institutional, Kaufman	491%
RS Funds Emerging Growth	480%
Dreyfus Founders	450%
WM Group NWest	444%
Liberty Acorn	443%
Fidelity Inv Growth	437%
American Funds A Growth	431%
One Group CI Mid Cap	417%
Oppenheimer	413%
Invesco Funds Dyn	411%
Seligman Captl A	403%
Delaware Class A Trend	390%
GS Elfun Trusts	387%
MFS Funds A Cap Opty	383%
Federate A Captl Apprc	381%
Brandywine	374%
MFS Funds A MA	374%
Parnassus Growth	374%
Alger Funds B Large Cap	371%
Gabelli Asset	368%
Dow Jones Industrials Average	352%

in 1990, and keep in mind this is not the most spectacularly performing market average, you would have had a compound gain of 352 percent. My point is that nine of the 25 top-performing funds barely exceeded a buy-and-hold strategy in the Dow. Keep in mind that we're looking at the best funds here—the ones that did the very best job of selecting growth stocks. Of the thousands and thousands of funds, only a handful were able to just keep up with the U.S. stock market itself! Only a select few were able to make much of a difference beyond a buy-and-hold strategy in the Dow. I think there are about 3,000 active mutual funds, so the table shown here tells us that only a minuscule number of the funds, of those guys looking for the highfliers, were able to beat the averages. The brightest of the brightest barely outshone the averages!

If the professionals can't catch the highfliers, I don't think you and I can, either. But what we can do is seek quality, seek value, and we will be rewarded.

Being successful in this business of investing, then, is all about having clear intentions with a single purpose in mind. That purpose is focused on the correct time frame for your investments as well as the correct vehicle for those investments. There'll be many sideshow attractions to lure you away from your purpose. In the heat of the moment you'll see stocks you wished you owned, and you'll be upset that somebody is making money when you are not doing as well. Someone will always be outperforming you, but let's see where that person is six months or a year or two from now, because today's darlings usually turn into next year's dogs.

Dreams of investment success are shadows in a game that's all about reality. Maintain your intentions, focus your purpose and you will find stock market success.

7

HOW TO SUPERCHARGE YOUR INVESTMENT RETURN

The opposite of any generally accepted idea is worth a fortune to somebody.

—Francis Scott Fitzgerald Key

Most investors get it all wrong: They think investing is about finding one or two hot stocks or a great piece of real estate, buy it, then cash out for a huge gain. That's not how money is really made in the world of investments. Far from it, this is a business of getting a return on your money. It is a business of making an amount of money worth more later than it is now. It is not about finding one-hit wonders or stocks that may zoom up in the future.

That, as we have seen earlier, is very much a game of Russian roulette. It's a bit like baseball—home run hitters strike out a lot. Isn't it interesting that despite the huge success of Mark McGwire, Sammy Sosa, and Barry Bonds when it comes to hitting home runs, their teams don't get to or win the World Series? They don't even win their divisions. So much for home runs! While they are spectacular and awesome things to see, almost as awesome as a stock that triples or quadruples in a six-month period, investing in this fashion becomes very much a hit-or-miss approach. You will strike out. Lots. And that's an expensive thing to do in this business. In baseball you get to bat again, but that may not be so easy for an investor.

In their search for investment profits people focus on the spectacular, forgetting that the way to long-term objectives is reached by having a campaign of action that includes goals, a theoretical understanding of what you hope to achieve, and a precise way of accomplishing those goals.

In this chapter I would like to help you construct a battle plan for investment survival.

FIRST RULE

Hopefully, by now you have realized the folly of trying to catch highfliers, or holding on forever to "growth stocks." If the funds can't do it, and few of them do, it will be nearly impossible for us to consistently find these runaway stocks. The entire approach to investing in these stocks, or so-called opportunities, basically revolves around stories and rumors, or noticing stocks that have gone up a great deal in anticipation they will go higher.

Trying to find such stocks is hardly an approach to investing; it is more like gambling. You are not purchasing stocks, you are purchasing hopes, high ones at that, and these hopes are usually based more on hype and investors' froth than anything substantial. In short, there simply is no methodology to this type of investment. I say this because in all my studies I have found there is absolutely nothing that consistently selects the highfliers that keep flying.

Most often, just about the time we buy the highflier, an engine conks out, a wing falls off, and our hard-earned cash goes up in flames.

This is very much a short-term approach to investing. It has nothing to do with a consistent application of proven investment techniques or strategies that we know make money. The major error I made when I first began trading and investing in stocks was to be attracted by these highfliers. I believed it was possible to find them, buy them, and hold on a short time to make seemingly instant wealth. The reality was that I was not able to do that and have not found anyone else who has consistently done it, either. Hot stocks are very random. I have learned to get rid of randomness in my life. Random success is accompanied by just as much random failure. Keep in mind that if the great minds and computers of Wall Street could do this they would have much better performance than they do.

Successful investing is all about having an advantage. My favorite parallel of this would be the casinos in Las Vegas. I assume you have been there or have seen pictures of this amazing town, which now possesses miniature mock-up replicas of all of the world's wonders with the exception of the Great Wall of China. I suppose the next thing they will build there will be a reconstruction of the tower of Babel. Then again, that may be there now.

How do you suppose those buildings, those fantastic hotels and dens of iniquity, were financed? "Oh, I know," you reply. "It was done from the losings of would-be gamblers, people who think they can beat the house." That is absolutely true. Gamblers are very much hit-or-miss investors. They're trying to catch a winner in a game were the odds are against them. Yes, sometimes they succeed, but since the casinos keep building more monstrosities, it suggests to us the casinos are the ones who bank on consistency.

So how do they do it? It's really quite simple; they have a game wherein they have a slight advantage ranging from 1.5 percent all way up to a 5 percent advantage. The average advantage is somewhere around 2.5 percent for most of their games of chance. "Games of chance," I like that; that's what catching highfliers is, a game of chance.

A 2.5 percent advantage doesn't turn on most investors. That's because they operate on an emotional basis where they think the way to bulk up investment return is by getting spectacular gains.

Instead, these people should listen to what Albert Einstein said: that he thought the most amazing thing in the world was compounding numbers. Let me give you an example of this.

We have two investors. One has a very good long-term investment program that yields 7.1 percent per year, while the other investor has a program that does a little bit better at 10.0 percent per year. At first blush you might think there won't be much difference in the net results these two investors will have—after all, the difference in yield is less than 3 percent per year. However, because of the magic of compounding over 60 years (a little longer than most of us will be or want to be investing, but it proves the point), the investor getting 7.1 percent a year will have turned $10,000 into $6 million. He'll be a happy guy until he finds that his neighbor with a slightly higher rate of return on the same amount of money, $10,000 in both cases, has ended up with a staggering $34 million.

That tiny little 2.9 percent difference, because of the mathematics of compounding, made $28 million more than the 7.1 percent return. Why does this happen? Simply because the compounding effect is gargantuan. Notice that neither investor had a particularly phenomenal rate of return, so it was not the investment strategy that made either of them wealthy, nearly as much as *it was the consistency of an approach* that was followed on a long-term basis and boosted up thanks to the compounding effect.

What this tells us, then, is that if we wish to maximize the return on our money we don't need a huge advantage in the game. We don't have to have 100 percent returns, year after year, to beat the pants off the stock market. We don't need excessive risk to succeed.

Most investors have unrealistic goals that can never be reached. Thus, they lose interest as well as their money. The approach I suggest is one that recognizes the reality of how difficult it is to catch hot stocks or to make money off of hot tips and rumors. The reality of investing is that we don't need to expose ourselves to these risks or capture the gains to be wildly successful in this business.

THE BEST INVESTMENT GOAL

Our goal, then, is not about making a killing on any one individual decision. Our goal is to develop an approach that consistently makes money and then consistently use that approach. If we beat the averages, we beat 80 percent of the brightest minds on Wall Street, and can make a fortune over time. I'm happy with that!

So how is all this accomplished?

There are really only two aspects to this type of investing.

The first is to find stocks that have a distinct tendency to outperform the market, to rally, to reward investors.

The second is to identify the most appropriate times when these stocks will rally.

While it is very popular to read in investment books that timing your entry into the markets is likely a waste of time, I totally disagree.

In the three years of 1999, 2000, and 2001, more than 60 percent of the stocks on the Nasdaq declined in value. In other words, you had only a 40 percent chance of getting a stock that went up. Over at the New York Stock Exchange we found better odds, but not much better. In the year 2000 about 58 percent of those stocks posted gains, and 42 percent went lower. In 2001, only 55 percent of the New York Stock Exchange issues advanced, cutting your odds of finding a winner even more.

It really gets down to this: Stocks are much better buys when the major market indexes are inclined to rally. It's just like the old adage says: Don't confuse brains with a bull market. A bull market bails out almost every investment error we can make.

When you consider the above percentages, keep in mind they are just percentage tabulations of how many stocks were up or down and have nothing to do with the magnitude of the move, which is even more important. Consider this: You buy 55 stocks that go up and 45 that go down. That looks like a winning scenario, but you'd lose money if the downers lost more than the uppers gained.

So, then, we have a two-pronged investment goal: Besides finding stocks that are likely to outperform, we must seek out the most opportune times when on an overall basis we expect stocks to rally, which I believe I've done to a large extent for you with our cyclical analysis.

Most likely we will not call the exact lows of many market moves, but it is just as likely that we will be on the sidelines during bear markets, during times when other investors are exposed to risk.

There are other tools you can use that will most likely have you investing at what is a market low point. The seasonal tendency of the stock market is extremely powerful, and I believe that can and should be one of your first considerations. I see little reason for investors to be fully invested during the months stocks have been most likely to decline and have posted major market crashes. By and large, that's from March through October. That is a high-risk time period for investors. By sitting on the sidelines during this time you will miss major market moves. Big deal! Consider the consequences of a crash that takes away 50 percent of the value of your holdings. That means the market must now stage a 100 percent rally to get you back to being even. That's a tough scenario—why expose yourself to it?

October is such a fascinating month. While it is a very bad month to come in on the long side, it has been a very good month to go out of on the long side. The one thing that will most influence your ability to make money in the market will be your success in sidestepping market declines. They are the bugaboo we need to protect ourselves from, the monster hiding in the dark shadows cast by all those Wall Street skyscrapers. If we can simply avoid one or two, if not the majority of market slides, we will substantially outperform all other investors.

I have shown you when most of these market slides occur, so why put ourselves in a place where trouble is most likely to find us? It boggles my mind why investors stay fully invested at times trouble is most likely to occur. These people would certainly not stand in front of a speeding freight train, yet have no reluctance to have all their money invested at the worst possible times.

I am always amused to see investors who are so meticulous about the issues they select to buy yet have no knowledge of market timing. But timing can make a huge difference. The first part of my investment strategy is to align with the major cyclical up moves in stock prices. We need to focus on this; we need to pay attention to it. It needs to be as much, part and parcel, of our investment strategy as what issues we select to invest in.

Your first lesson, then, is to focus your investment decisions at these times and only at these times, as opposed to being fully invested 100 percent of the time. I believe one reason funds have not been able to beat the market averages is that due to their size they can't get out at times, even if they wanted to.

We have a distinct advantage over the funds in that regard. We can pull our punches, wait until we think we are at opportune buying times or zones. We certainly don't expect to call all the swings of the marketplace, but we do expect—and it is a reasonable expectation—to generally make our purchases at times the stock market is most likely to rally in the ensuing 12 months. Timing does make a difference; long-term studies show perfect timing can almost triple your rate of return. But again, the emphasis there is on perfect timing, a difficult thing to accomplish.

The final lesson is that the business of investing is a long-range approach. Once you determine your basic battle plan, stick with it. Just as to stay in good physical condition one needs to exercise on a consistent basis, so it is with capital appreciation of your money. You need to set time aside on a weekly or monthly basis so that you can follow your plan of action. If you don't follow a plan of action, why make a plan of action? This is serious business here; this is about money, your money. Your ability to enhance the return on your money will be directly proportional to the consistent application of your strategy.

Trust me on this. The markets are not always easy; they will test what you are made of; they continually put your emotions up against a wall. At times like these most investors fold, or switch horses midstream. When under pressure it is amazing what the human mind can dredge and dream up. You will rationalize that the strategy doesn't work anymore, though the strategies have worked for almost 100 years. Yet at any given point in time they may falter. That is to be expected.

Let's talk about that.

To me our objective is to beat the stock market averages. If we can do that on a consistent basis we come out way ahead. Thus if the stock market is down we may, if we're fortunate, be slightly up or marginally down. At times we may underperform the stock market itself. Continuing with my Las Vegas analogy, please keep this point foremost in your thinking: At any given time in every casino of the world, the house will have a losing streak. Some lucky punter will be winning.

How do the casinos handle that? Do they shut down the tables? Do they come in and decide to make new rules? Of course not! Why would they do that? They know they have a game where they will come out ahead in the long run, which is why they consistently spin the wheel, deal the cards, and roll the dice. While they do not like anyone taking their money, any more than you like a stock declining against you, it is not a reason to change the game, to invent a strategy radically different from what has been proven to be so successful in the past.

There are really two parts to correct action in this part of our investment strategy. The impeccable warrior, and that is such a great way to think of yourself in this game of investments, will go to war only when it is the correct time to wage war and will consistently use proven strategies. It really gets down to the hard work and drudgery of repetitive action. People don't like repetitive action, especially investors. They want exciting action, big up moves, thrills—all those things that are destined to lead to . . . spills.

Our secret of success is the consistent application of doing the right thing. Do it for a long enough time period and you're bound to find success. You can't avoid it; it will happen.

OUR SECOND GOAL

It's time to get down to work now, to show you how an investor can accomplish an advantage in selecting individual issues. Our strategy, then, would be to combine general, overall, market timing with a superior selection strategy. Our goal is to find stocks where we have a distinct advantage that they will rally. Our selection process deliberately, and consciously, does not attempt to catch the uncatchable or delve into the dream stocks that have become the downfall of so many investors.

In the next chapter I'm going to present to you numerous strategies that have been proven by a tremendous amount of research, as well as real-time investing, to give us an advantage in the game . . . to put us one step ahead other investors. You don't have to be particularly intelligent to be successful in this business. Hard work and native intelligence will carry the day for an investor.

Success in the business world, probably in the entire world, comes from being smart. Being smart, or smarter than the next guy, is the product of studying and learning. Being successful, or more successful than the next guy, is the product of the application of what you've learned.

8

THE OLD ECONOMY IS THE NEW ECONOMY

Historians ponder the past; investors ponder the future.
. . . One is more profitable than the other.

"The new economy"—it was supposed to solve all the problems of mankind. Sales and marketing, along with virtually all levels of corporate existence, were to be radically changed—changed forever. The rules of the past were to have been tossed out, as we were promised sweeping new innovations that would make life easier and investors much richer.

It was same song, same dance to me. I had heard this "new world" concept in the 1960s, and then again in the 1970s. Each time, shortly thereafter, the stock market crashed. As the French say, "The more things change the more they stay the same." In the new economy the lessons and rules from the past supposedly didn't matter. Stocks were to be valued not by what the companies did, but rather by *what they might do in the future.* Suddenly stocks were selling at 100 times earnings—some all the way up to 200 times. Sad to say, many investors lost a substantial part of their money, in many instances actual fortunes, all because they did not pay attention to one simple little number—the price-earnings ratio. It was telling investors it would take 200 years for the company to earn enough money to justify the current price of one share of stock!

Talk about being long-term investors; the short-term speculators were betting on a 200-year hold.

"Momentum," that's what it was all about they said. The new breed of investors, who I think should be called punters, had run stock data through their computers to discover that stocks that went higher continued going higher. That was true because the overall market of the 1980s was in a gargantuan uptrend. Noticing this, the hotshot wizards from Harvard, Stanford, and the like used the same strategy of buying strong stocks. That lasted for awhile, just long enough for them to look really good. Hence, they acquired more money under management, so when the ultimate day of reckoning did come they did not lose just a little—they lost a lot.

As I have frequently said, "The reward of value may be delayed, but ultimately it cannot be denied." The opposite of that is equally true: Stocks may become overvalued and then become even more overvalued, but ultimately chickens come home to roost. There's never been a stock in history that has been able to consistently maintain a P/E ratio over 100 without a significant market collapse and decline in price. Never, ever, ball fans.

The price-earnings ratio has been with us for many years. As a young man I was told that whenever the Dow Jones Industrial Average sported a P/E ratio greater than 30 there was trouble ahead. Nowadays stocks can exceed that 30 reading, but in most cases not for long. What this ratio looks at is the price of the stock divided by the earnings the company is producing. The cool thing about this indicator is it deals with reality—it looks at the current price versus the current amount of money the company is earning. There's no conjecture here, no room for myth or hype, it simply is what it is. One simply divides the current price by the current earnings to arrive at this ratio.

It all starts with earnings, then, doesn't it? When companies are earning money they are appreciated by long-term investors much more than when earnings are negligible or nonexistent. It sounds ridiculously simple to ask this question: "Is the company you are investing in making money or not?" Had millions of investors had the gumption to ask just that one question about the highfliers of the high-tech new economy, I suspect they would never have put down a single nickel for all those stocks that lost all that money. Why didn't they ask that question? is my question.

The answer is simple: They got so carried away with the up move in individual prices that they simply threw all caution to the winds. Reality didn't matter; after all, we were in a new economy, with new rules. The law of gravity had been repealed. The economic laws had also, apparently, been revoked. There was a short circuit of the logical process as prices went to astronomical levels for no reason at all. Investors kept dancing to the sound of the piper's music, buying and buying, chasing strength.

All that has changed now. The piper came to be paid. A July 2001 *Wall Street Journal* article was headlined, "Merrill's Recent Picks Are Strong on Stability." Value stocks have substantially outperformed growth stocks was the point of the article. I think we are going to see a whole lot more of this investment strategy in the future as brokerage firms and investment advisers return to the fundamentals of value.

Bob Doll, from Merrill Lynch, expressed it this way: "We're shooting for earnings visibility." Considering the size of Merrill's operation—some $57 billion in assets in 48 funds—one gets a sense of the impact this change in the investment community may make on individual issues.

HOW TO KNOW WHAT THE FUNDS ARE DOING

You can follow what these large institutional firms are buying each Friday. That's the day *Investor's Business Daily* reveals the 25 largest stock positions for the largest mutual funds. This is an excellent way of seeing what stocks these funds are holding and may be a good place for you to look for long-term stocks to run through our various value models. Notice that the newspaper places the capital letter N next to a new position a fund has taken since the last reporting period. Additionally, you'll find a plus or minus to indicate whether the fund is adding to the position or selling off part of it. This can be an extremely important reference, not only for seeing how your stocks are doing, but also as a quick and easy way to spot potential investment candidates.

As an example, a recent listing shows the largest accumulation of individual stocks by Merrill Lynch had been Bristol-Myers Squibb, Home Depot, and PepsiCo. The largest sells were Citigroup, Verizon, and Pfizer. There is additional information that we can also quickly discover, thanks to the newspaper. An investor is clearly shown the industries where these funds are making their largest bets. This may focus our attention on a particular industry. In this tabulation, the largest investment by the funds under Merrill Lynch's control was in the medical-ethical drugs industry with some $153 million of new money pouring in. The retail/wholesale industry was a distant second with an influx of $97 million of new money.

THERE ARE ONLY TWO REASONS A STOCK GOES UP

As near as I can tell, there are only two reasons for a stock to advance. The first is that the company gains some type of popularity or notoriety. This is fodder for reports and stories of new prospects, potential gains. People love new things, love innovations; investors are always looking for the newest innovation in the marketplace on the assumption that it will drive prices higher. Stocks have rotated over the years. One year the drug stocks were in vogue and simply couldn't go down. That was until another group of stocks, the biogenetic ones, became the darlings of the day, which gave way to computer chip manufacturers. And so it continues; there's always one group of stocks that just caught investors' fancy.

These stocks go up because of stories and rumors and possibly even some form of manipulation, which is not out of question in a free market system. When people are long stocks it is only natural for them to want prices to go higher. Some people just may want to see if they can be part of that program through a campaign of positive publicity, which may even deteriorate into out-and-out touting. Trust me, it happens. I've seen it—it takes place. I know it is not supposed to, but it does. There are even legal forms of this, after all, corporations can run ads, and investors can have their brokers call up suggesting you and I purchase stocks based on the stories they spin. Brokers would make good politicians, as they are wonderful spin doctors.

Everyone seeks the same outcome; then at some point, higher prices themselves become what is driving the stock higher. A feeding frenzy has begun. The beast feeds upon itself! To the surprise of classical economists, higher prices, which are supposed to deter or decrease demand, have in actuality increased demand. Computer bells have sounded the alarm; the gargantuan momentum or up move appears to be precisely a promise of profitable performance for the coming good years. Sometimes that scenario works out, at least for a while, but most often what runs up like a balloon full of hot air falls once investors' attention is turned in another direction or some pundit bursts the balloon.

That's why stocks such as Priceline.com could rally from $10 a share to $105 a share and back down to $5 a share, and all in less than 15 months. This stock is not an exception—I have seen it happen time and time again. Which means it will happen in the future, many more times.

News stories and/or the great myth of a revolutionary new product or market have driven up the price of a stock. You should never underestimate the ability of news and greed to drive prices higher.

THE SECOND REASON STOCKS ADVANCE

The second reason stocks go up, and certainly the more stable one, is because the company is making money. What a novel concept this is: Make money and the price of the stock goes higher! There are several ways of looking at earnings ratios and that sort of thing, but one of the most significant ways I think of using them is to see whether the earnings are erratic or consistent. I'm certain you have figured it out; investors would prefer consistency that eliminates questions and fear of the future. The market hates the unknown; it hates anything that is unreliable. So an erratic pattern of earnings may occur in a stock that has a short-term rally, but this is not where serious and consistent (as well as easy) money is to be made.

As earnings go, so go the prices of stocks. That is our mantra, now and forever. You can have your choice: Buy stocks that go up on the whims of news and stories or ones that go up based on actual conditions.

It's your choice: news or value? I have chosen value, as you will see. The mantra of value can become a most valuable tool in helping us make our individual stock market selections. The all-time great long-term growth stocks maintained their price advances, in just about every instance, only during times when they were consistently profitable and were becoming more so every single quarter.

The great stocks of the past, when they did collapse, clearly started their declines about the time their earnings started to decline. Thus, this is one of the most important facets of investing, one of the best indicators we can follow.

HOW TO BUY STOCKS AT A "DISCOUNT"

Because of stories, rumors, news, and overall market conditions, even good stocks, those with consistent increases in earnings, can and do go down. I have determined a rather unique way of telling when it is best to purchase these stocks when they are at what I would call a "discount."

The discount I'm talking about is the discount in relation to their earnings. The pattern we will be looking for is one of consistent increases in earnings—which means that the current 12 months earnings number is greater than that reported at the accounting period three months earlier. What's going on here is the company is still making money and still increasing its earnings growth. That's good.

However, for one reason or another—usually overall market conditions, I should point out—the price of the stock enters a declining phase. The farther the stock declines, the more it approaches being at a "discount," if you will, to the trend of its earnings.

What's going on here is that while prices of the stock have been declining, the overall conditions of the company have been improving, as evidenced by an increase in earnings. This is a very positive divergence: price down, earnings up. Unfortunately, this condition doesn't occur very often in the life of a stock; but when it does it usually marks one of the most opportune times to step in and buy, and buy in the face of price weakness!

I'm showing several examples so you can see for yourself how powerful this technique is. All the following show price action versus earnings. You can see this technique in action in almost any charting service that shows earnings as well as price action. I strongly suggest you subscribe to a financial newspaper so that you can get a feel for this technique of locating stocks that are undervalued in relation to their earnings growth. Financial newspapers frequently print charts of stocks and their earnings. While most investors look at all sorts of things, ratios and the like, I simply want to find a stock that is priced lower this quarter than the prior quarter. The key is that at the same time earnings are higher this quarter than the prior quarter.

Such a pattern of divergence sets up our buy signal. You can enter simply at the end of the quarter, or, if one wanted to play things a little closer to the vest, perhaps have a buy order slightly above the market price to make certain the trend has turned up.

Harley-Davidson

Harley-Davidson has been one of the premier growth stocks, and there's an obvious reason why. Check out the earnings trend shown in Figure 8.1. Quarter after quarter, year after year, the company has managed to increase its earnings per share. This is the ideal scenario investors should see. The company is almost impervious to downturns in its earnings. They have consistently done better—what a great sign that is to long-term investors!

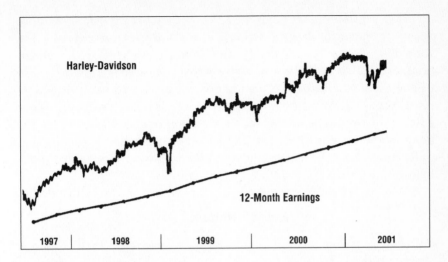

Figure 8.1 Harley-Davidson

But notice the price of the stock does not necessarily travel in a straight line upward. Indeed, look at what happened in 1999: Prices stalled out at the $32 share level, dipping down to $23 a share. Or how about the wild ride in the third quarter of 1998 when prices went from $20 to $13? I'll bet that scared most of the riders of this stock off their Harley "hogs." We, however, would have seen it differently. We would have noticed that at the same time earnings were better at the end of the third quarter of the year despite the decline in stock prices, just as they had been at the end of the last quarter in 1997. Prices had declined from approximately $16 a share to $12 a share, setting up the buy signal, and away went Harley. The next point to be a buyer of the stock was on the decline into the start of the fourth quarter in 1998.

The increase in earnings while the stock was declining was a give-away as an indication of higher prices to come. The next time this oc-curred was in June 1999 when prices were marginally lower for the quarter. The price of Harley didn't do much following this juncture. However, the same scenario developed at the start of the last quarter of 1999, when again prices got slammed down but earnings continued churning forward. That was your fourth opportunity to buy the stock, this time at about $24 a share.

That began a move taking the stock to $46 a share before the price again got slammed, declining from $50 a share back down to the $35 zone. But once more, our handy dandy internal view of market conditions, earnings, was still in a positive up trend, suggesting the stock could be purchased at a discount. After all, prices were down and earnings were up. That buy signal at $34 looked pretty good, as prices had moved above $50 a share since. The start of the third quarter in 2001 looked like a buy point as the price of the stock had been flat if not down, yet earnings again continued to be higher, suggesting the stock was undervalued in the $36 a share area.

Federal Home Loan

It's a long step from motorcycles to mortgage companies. Their corporate enterprises have precious little, if anything, in common. But when it comes to investor interest, the same thing continues to work when earnings are increasing and the price of the stock is down. Historically, the stock has been a buy. The first setup we see in Figure 8.2 was in the September 1998 time. The price declined for the quarter yet earnings were higher than the prior quarter. The stock rallied. Buy signals continued to

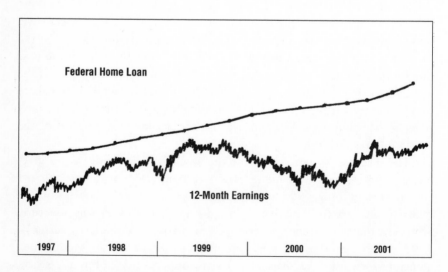

Figure 8.2   Federal Home Loan

develop as I've marked on the chart in September 1999, December 1999, March 2000, and as well as June 2000. Your average cost would have been approximately $46 a share. It was not until September 2000 the market seemed to notice this discrepancy or discount. Keep in mind that the reward of value may be delayed but it is never denied. A year later you could have cashed out almost doubling your money as the stock began trading near $70 a share.

It was such an obvious play; consecutive increases in earnings are extremely positive to the long-term trend of individual stocks. Traders and investors may not notice this for a while, which is why we want to carefully follow this earnings-to-price relationship. But at some point the dam breaks and the price moves higher.

Hillenbrand Industries

There are countless examples of this discount buying opportunity developing in stock after stock. I chose one at random here in a company I know nothing about, Hillenbrand Industries. If we studied just the price action of this stock from 1984 into 1998 (see Figure 8.3) we might suspect it was one of the computer or new economy issues. But it's not. Hillenbrand is

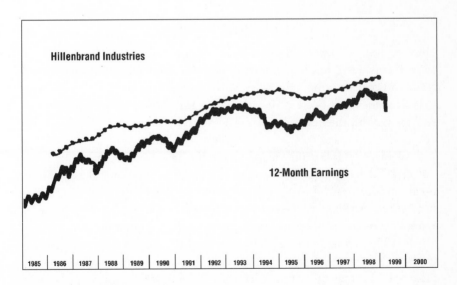

Figure 8.3 Hillenbrand Industries

primarily engaged in funeral services. See, you don't have to be involved in high tech to make money.

Notice how consistently the price mirrored earnings. As earnings increase, the price increases. That is the law of the Wall Street jungle.

But along the way, at times, the price has declined. Notably, look at the decline in the fall of 1987. Look as well at what earnings were doing, though; they were increasing, telling us that the stock was a buy in the $10 area. Earnings were slightly higher in 1990, while the last two quarters of that year saw prices declining. This again sets up our discount buying opportunity. In 1993 an investor would not have done quite so well, as earnings went higher while the price went lower, thus setting up a buy point in the $40 a share area. No rally sprang up, but as long as earnings were going higher we would know we were getting the stock at a discount. This condition—increased earnings as lower prices continued into 1994 when the stock bottomed at $26 a share, still giving our discount bottom buy signal—may well be one of the reasons the stock zoomed up to $64 a share, more than doubling in the next to 18 months.

Again, a discount buying opportunity was presented. Earnings continued going up during time periods when the stock price went down. Each and every example of this discount buying opportunity would have made money for the savvy investor.

Carlisle Companies

Here is another one of those nondescript companies, not much glamour to it. Carlisle is a holding company with interests in automotive, industrial, and construction materials. Yet look what the price did (see Figure 8.4). It went from $6 to $50 a share. Again, there's no need to get carried away with the new economy. The old economy, thank you, has done very well.

An investor following this issue would have noticed that as it broke out in 1992 to the upside it was in some type of uptrend. Prices did not break out of the 1984 to 1992 base because of the chart. No, prices broke out because earnings broke out to the upside as the company began seven years of consecutive increases in its annualized earnings reports.

In 1994 earnings substantially increased yet the price moved sideways in the $16 zone. This presented us with a discount buying opportunity— price flat, earnings up. Guess what else. It was 1994—right in phase with our four-year phenomenon, which led, in this case, to a decennial pattern

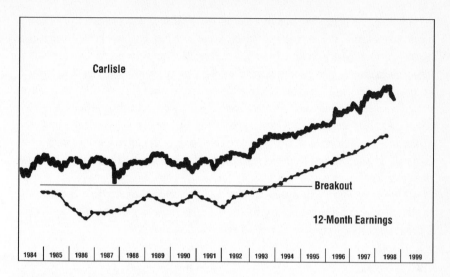

Figure 8.4 Carlisle Companies

five year, when one usually sees bull markets. The stock responded in stellar fashion, continuing to rally.

In the first quarter of 1996 there was another discount buying opportunity as well as one in the second quarter of 1997 that set up a buy point in the $27 range. Astute investors purchasing at this time period because of the discount scenario were quickly rewarded with an increase of prices to over $50 a share.

Chartists and technicians spend their entire lives looking at price structures trying to divine in some fashion what the future might be. What a futile experience, what a waste of time! Charts are next to impossible to read, daily or weekly price action are a mumbo jumbo of chickenlike scratches on paper.

The significance of price charts comes not from looking at prices but from looking at what causes prices to move, which is, by and large, earnings.

Thompson Corp.

Let's now turn our attention to Thompson Corp., a publishing company of travel and financial-related materials. While our chartist and technician friends look at price, we are interested in earnings. It takes no more than a glance at Figure 8.5 to see that this company has had an erratic earnings history and has not been able to consistently make money. Does a stock like this excite us? No way! Turn the page, hang up on your broker, cancel your subscription to the newsletter that recommends stocks like this. Sure, it had a nice price move from $12 all the way to $30, but stocks like this can crash just as easily as they rally. The inconsistency of earnings is a killer. It is far easier and more secure to invest in companies that have consistently made money than to fool around with stocks that move because of the unexplained.

Always keep in mind that charts do not move the market's conditions; fundamental conditions move the market the majority of the time and with a great deal more consistency than technical gibberish.

GOING BEYOND EARNINGS: COMPANY DEBT

Earnings are not the only thing I pay attention to but they certainly are the most dominant focus. Later on we will get to things like dividends, yields,

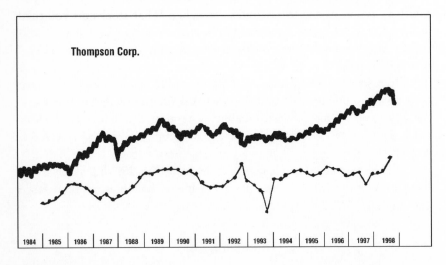

Figure 8.5 Thompson Corp.

and the all-important price-to-sales ratios. But before we get there, let's talk about two other important considerations that help us select great stocks: company debt and insider buying and selling.

When I look at the balance sheet of a company, in addition to its earnings I am very interested in looking at the amount of debt the company has. I do not like debt; I do not like it in my life, and I don't like it in corporate life. I've been in debt, and I've been out of debt. Being out is far better, I assure you.

There two problems with debt: On a personal basis it is simply the pressure it places on us. Can you imagine what is like to be a corporate CEO knowing you are on the hook, or the company is, for hundreds of millions of dollars? I suggest a CEO in that scenario is not as flexible, or creative, or productive as the CEO who doesn't owe one penny to the bankers.

So, one CEO is simply better off psychologically than the other. If you believe, as I do, much of our success in life starts from our belief system or our attitude, this is a tremendously important consideration. I'm convinced some CEOs have so much debt that they just can't envision ever liquidating it, so they, and their companies, simply muddle along paying the piper and getting noplace.

The inherent problem with debt has to do with a poor economy. As we know, the stock market is not a straight road up; it also goes down. It usually goes down when interest rates go higher. What stocks do you think will go down most when interest rates go higher?

Obviously, stocks of companies that have substantial debt will go down most, simply because the corporations must now pay a greater percentage of their income to the bankers. This doesn't leave them funds left over to expand their companies and/or pay dividends to shareholders.

Not only does this place restrictions on the companies, but it places further psychological pressures on those running these high-rolling outfits. The CEOs have no choice but to pay the bankers, because if they don't pay the financial institutions, the loans are called in, and the prices of the stocks suffer even more. So the first allegiance is not to shareholders, nor is the first allegiance to the companies themselves, which could use that money to further promote their products and/or expand their operation and research abilities. The bankers come first.

Our second mantra of investing is "stay away from high-debt companies." Buy low debt/no debt companies. When the times get tough those guys don't get beaten up nearly as much as the highballing, high debt puffed up companies.

WOULD YOU EAT THERE? INSIDER BUYING AND SELLING

Let's forget about stock investing for moment and talk about food. Let's talk about eating in a very nice restaurant, perhaps the nicest one in town. If you saw the owners of that restaurant taking their meals, on a daily basis, at the restaurant across the street, what would you think? Would you think something was wrong? The people who own a restaurant are afraid to eat at their own place?

I would! It is no different when it comes to the world of finance. One of the better long-term indicators of potential growth in a company comes from monitoring the purchases and sales of the stock of the people who work at the company. It makes ultimate sense; if the people who work there are buying stock in the company it most likely is going to rally. They believe in the company, believe in it so much they are plunking down their hard-earned cash.

The other side of this issue is if the people who work there are selling their stock, getting out of the market, one just might suspect there's a reason for this. Now, what could that reason be? And who would know better if the stock was going up or down than the people who work there?

One of the realities of the marketplace is that insiders have an extremely good record of getting out of their companies the right time and buying into their companies the right time. One of the best all-time trades in the history of mankind was that by Bill Gates.

People give Gates all sorts of credit for being a computer whiz kid and an iconoclastic, positively brilliant businessman. They see him as the type of genius who has visions of a future that we have not yet begun to grasp. All that could be so, but it is not what impresses me most. What impresses me most about Bill Gates is that he had the foresight to sell thousands and thousands and thousands of shares of his Microsoft stock when it was trading at about $100 a share, just before it plunged to $40 a share. He is the best trader in history, making hundreds of millions upon millions of dollars of real profits based on his timely selling.

The numbers of his trade were staggering (see Figure 8.6). On February 22, 2000, he liquidated 2.9 million shares. His good buddy, Paul Allen, who had began selling off Microsoft in the fall of 1999, sold 164 million

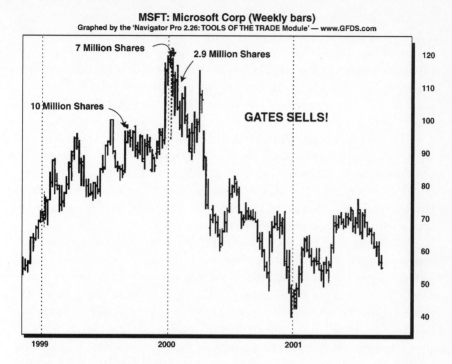

MSFT: Microsoft Corp (Weekly bars)
Graphed by the 'Navigator Pro 2.26: TOOLS OF THE TRADE Module' — www.GFDS.com

Figure 8.6   Microsoft Corporation 1999–2001

shares on February 11, 2000. When one looks at their activity at this time it appears they spent more time with their brokers to liquidate stocks than with corporate activity. They just sold and sold!

In some fashion, and for some reason, whatever that was, they got out of the market just before the big slide began. Smart guys do smart things. The owners of companies, especially the size of Microsoft, are smart. When they do things they are most likely to be correct, and history shows it behooves us to follow their action.

An insight here into insider buying and selling is that if just one investor in the company is buying or selling, it is not nearly as significant as if a group of the insiders is purchasing or selling. Any one individual may need to sell stock for tax purposes, to buy a new house, or whatever. But when a cluster of these people start liquidating their stocks it's a safe bet they're not all buying a new house. They all have probably seen some reason to take such action. The more insider buying and selling at a specific time, the stronger the message is.

Also, of course, the amount of stock they are selling is significant; an insider selling 100 shares is not as negative as an insider selling 1,000 shares. Insiders are required to report to the Securities and Exchange Commission all of their activity by the 10th of the month following the time they bought or sold. Sometimes these insiders will delay their purchase or sales the maximum amount of time to just get under the filing requirement.

The level of insider selling almost always exceeds that of insider buying, so we need to monitor the selling in light of the fact many corporate executives are compensated by stock as well as salaries. Generally speaking, there are about 2.5 shares of insider selling for every share of insider buying. Looking at that ratio may help you understand what is going on in the companies you are interested in.

Fortunately, we can track insider buying and selling activity for free on the Internet. My favorite web site is www.insiderreview.com. There is as much information as one could possibly want about insider transactions on this web site. You can select the stock of your choice with the ticker symbol or review all stocks that have been purchased and sold by insiders. There is also a tabulation of insider activity specifically designed to show you where the majority of buying and selling is currently being done.

Additionally, the web site offers the ability to follow the insiders who have the best record of buying and selling to give us further focus and help us use this approach to trading or investing. There are literally thousands of pages filed on a daily basis with the Securities and Exchange Commission, far more than you and I could ever go through, so it is simply wonderful to have all this information available at the click of a mouse.

Once you have found the stocks you are interested in, you may filter them out with some of my techniques, or perhaps screens from other authors or of your own making. I would suggest you go to the web site just to make certain insiders have not been dumping the stock you want to purchase. Hopefully, you will see they have been big buyers, or you may spot a different stock where insiders have been large accumulators. Good! Then check out its earnings, and so forth.

Let's review our big three fundamental guns to begin our search for great growth stocks. First we want to pay attention to earnings. We will pass on any company that is not making money and/or not doing it in a consistent fashion. We'll follow the money—show us that money is being earned and we will consider investing.

Then we'll run a background check on our potential investments to see what type of financial shape they are in. If they have a lot of debt, no thanks! Finally, if people who work there have been consistently selling off huge quantities of company stock they own, no thanks!

Yes, there is a great deal more information investors can look at for their selection techniques. What I have found, however, is so overwhelming that we do get bogged down in the details. The three points made in this chapter are just about all you need. Next is some refinement of our techniques and where and how to obtain the information.

9

MEASURING INVESTOR SENTIMENT FOR INDIVIDUAL STOCKS

Experience is a good teacher, but she sends terrific bills.
—Anonymous

The majority of short-term traders lose money. Is there a way to do the opposite of this? If the majority of traders are wrong the majority of the time, wouldn't it behoove us to do the opposite of what they do?

This is far from a new idea. Writing in the 1930s, Garfield Drew was most likely the first analyst to not only espouse this view but present a workable solution to the problem. Drew classified public investor activity into two categories: (1) customers' equity or cash balances at their brokers and (2) odd lot short sales.

The more enduring of these two indicators has been odd lot short sales. Since an odd lot, Drew reasoned, was less than 100 shares, such activity most likely represented the small investor, someone with not enough money to buy in the traditional 100-share increments.

For over 70 years this point has been proven correct; abnormally high levels of odd lot short sales occur at market lows, while a decline in odd lot short sales (thus indicating public bullishness) usually heralds market rises. It is a truism, but a sad one, that the majority of investors just can't seem to get it right.

But we can fade the majority because the majority of people are not rich.

Other analysts such as Wally Heiby, Richard Dysart, Marty Zweig, and Ned Davis have done additional work along this line. Their work has been regarding overall stock market timing. Perhaps most notable has been the Investors Intelligence service, which measures the sentiment of folks who write newsletters. For over 35 years the record of the hotshot newsletter writers has paralleled the public's inability to correctly forecast future activity.

Jim Sibbett, a commodity analyst and the original publisher of *Market Vane*, began recording the bullishness of newsletter writers on individual commodities in the late 1960s. His work showed that not only could sentiment data be used for overall market timing, but it also could be used for individual commodity timing.

His data is quite clear: All of the major commodity markets respond to too much adviser bullishness by declining, too little bullishness by rallying.

Sibbett's work was all done with weekly data. This changed when Jake Bernstein began measuring 50 traders' bullishness/bearishness on a daily basis.

His work on daily sentiment, on a list of widely followed commodities, drives home the same point; even on an individual and daily basis, investor sentiment can provide real insight into the next move in the marketplace.

HOW INVESTOR SENTIMENT IMPACTS INDIVIDUAL STOCKS

To further this concept I began measuring investor sentiment toward individual stocks, namely the 30 stocks in the Dow Jones Industrial Average plus a few of the most popular issues such as Qualcomm, Sun Microsystems, and Apple Computer.

Thanks to the Internet, it is now possible to track many, many advisers on a daily as well as weekly basis to cull out the majority opinion. Heretofore, this would have been almost impossible to do in a timely fashion. Now, with instant communication all over the world, it is possible to collect the views of the majority.

While the specific construction index I am about to show is proprietary, the general components are not. You could do this yourself if you had the resources and time. The index is arrived at by visiting web sites and print media to determine how many of the surveyed analysts are bullish. This value is then taken as a percent of all votes cast, thus giving a base or raw number of percent bullishness.

There is some smoothing of the data, but only after a technical measure of public bullishness has been tossed into the concoction. Instead of interviewing individual members of the trading public each day, we measure their mostly likely activity in the market as a percent of all market activity. This is a slightly different view of what I first began writing about in the 1960s in my work on accumulation and distribution. Put/call ratios also provide an important factor in the index.

These measures of daily activity are blended into the weekly readings.

What I discovered was as illuminating as it was confirmatory of what one would expect: Intermediate-term market highs are marked by high levels of investor optimism, while market lows are almost always accompanied by low levels of optimism.

René Descartes, the seventeenth-century French philosopher credited with the line, "I think, therefore I am," is perhaps the founding father of this philosophy as well. He apparently made his living gambling and, in addition to his pontifications on life, left us with this thought for speculators: "It is more likely the truth will have been discovered by the few rather than by the many."

In trader talk that means, "Just when the many have discovered the trend is up it is most likely to change."

So, whether it's Descartes' thought or Garfield Drew's work, Marty Zweig's, or mine, a truth of market activity has been uncovered or at least confirmed: You can fade the uninformed investor or majority view most of the time.

LET THE EVIDENCE SPEAK FOR ITSELF

Figures 9.1, 9.2, and 9.3 depict sentiment on weekly charts. As you can see, I have marked off the excessive bullish levels with a reading over 75 percent, while market lows are most likely to take place with 25 percent or less of our survey sample looking to be buyers.

Our Basic Rule

The first rule, if you will, is that these zones of excessive bullishness and bearishness are where prices usually reverse themselves. It is as Heraclitus said in 500 B.C.: "Every trend must go too far and evoke its own reversal."

As proof of this phenomenon, let's look at Figure 9.1 of J. P. Morgan from 1996 through the spring of 2000. I have marked off the excessive bullish and bearish areas. The vast majority lead to setting up profitable trades. This is, indeed, the rule rather than the exception.

Figure 9.2, of 3M, shows the same general observation to be true.

JPM/J.P. Morgan & Company (1996–2000, weekly)

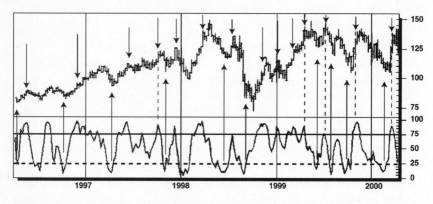

Figure 9.1   J.P. Morgan 1996–2000

MMM/Minnesota Mining & Manufacturing Company (1996–2000, weekly)

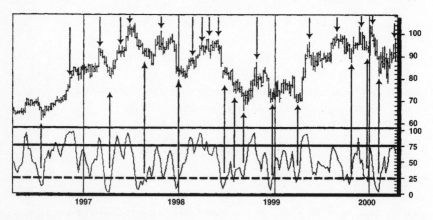

Figure 9.2   3M 1996–2000

MRK/Merck & Company Inc. (1996–2000, weekly)

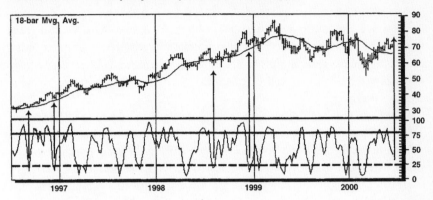

Figure 9.3   Merck 1996–2000

When the majority of advisers are too bullish, more than 75 percent of them, prices are more likely to decline than rally over the ensuing weeks.

By the same token, when the number of bullish advisers is less than 25 percent the odds of a market rally are greatly enhanced. Indeed, the most profitable rallies in these four years were all given birth by sentiment readings in the lower quartile, as I have marked off. The second law of thermodynamics in physics teaches that all things tend to go from an ordered state to a less ordered state. Disorder, or entropy, always increases.

That's pretty much what happens here. All that order of the trend, a decrease in the entropy of the common outlook, actually increases the entropy in another area, namely trend reversal.

Let's turn our attention to a disparate company, Merck (see Figure 9.3). It matters not what the company does—it can be banking like J. P. Morgan, a diversified technology company like 3M, or a drug stock like Merck. The rule of the jungle still prevails. Virtually all of the ideal buy and sell times in this stock from 1997 forward have coincided with our sentiment index being in the correct zone.

The problem is, there may be readings that do not produce major moves. The index did call just about all major highs and lows—that's the good news—but it gives a few signals that are not accurate. I will show one technique to avoid some of these, and you may have some techniques of your own.

HOW OPTION TRADERS CAN USE THE INDEX

Perhaps you are a long-term player in Merck. You own the stock but want to earn some extra income by writing puts and calls. The sentiment index can be of great value. Simply write puts when less than 25 percent of the advisers are bullish, and sell calls against your position when over 75 percent are bullish.

Perhaps you are following a stock you want to add to your portfolio. The only question in your mind is when will be the best time to buy. The sentiment index can come to your rescue! Why make your purchase of the stock when the majority has been buying, given the majority's record of most often doing the wrong thing? Simply wait until the weekly index dips into the 25 percent area or lower and then make your investment.

I have marked off some of the 25 perent zone buy points for your observation. Considering the mechanical simplicity of the technique, the results are truly remarkable.

Figure 9.4 shows buy arrows for this stock from 1993 into 2000. While not perfect (nothing in the real world of speculation is), it is awesome to see how many of the arrows denoted ideal entry points for the long-term acquisition of Merck, or, if you owned the stock, precise points to write puts so you would get the income without the stock being taken away.

No longer do you need to throw darts; instead, track the dart throwers!

MRK/Merck & Company Inc. (1993–1997, weekly)

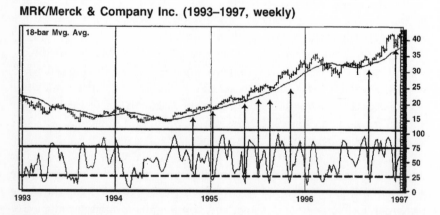

Figure 9.4 Merck 1993–1997

America's love affair with Microsoft came to an end in the year 2000, largely due to government action. Countless families lost millions of dollars thanks to the judicial and bureaucratic attitude of "I'm from the government and am here to help you. The most successful entrepreneur in the country's history must have cheated; how else could he have succeeded?"

Interestingly enough, however, our fade-the-crowd rule was alive and working. The sentiment index stood at 77 percent the week prior to the largest decline in the company's history (see Figure 9.5). Indeed, most of the major moves have been clearly indicated by the excessive bullishness and bearishness of our favorite group of advisers.

This is not a new phenomenon. In Figure 9.6, which shows Microsoft from 1992 to 1995, the same pattern of excess was at work. What we are really seeing here is the natural cycle of a pendulum swinging from everyone believing the trend is one way to no one believing.

Speculation is largely the art of doing what others are not, when they think they are doing what they ought to be doing.

WHAT MAKES THE ADVISERS TOO BULLISH AND TOO BEARISH?

The evidence is pretty convincing, as you have seen. But why is this so? What is the function behind the index?

The driving force of the index is what the market has been doing. The

MSFT/Microsoft Corporation (1997–2000, weekly)

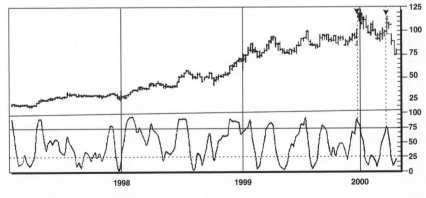

Figure 9.5   Microsoft 1997–2000

MSFT/Microsoft Corporation (1992–1995, weekly)

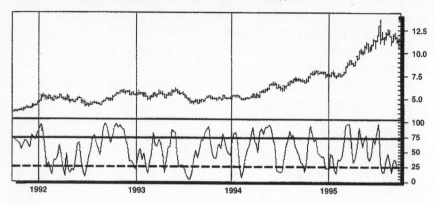

Figure 9.6   Microsoft 1992–1995

stronger and longer a rally is, the more bullish these folks become. Only one thing makes these folks bullish, it appears: a strong market rally. Only one thing makes them turn bearish: a decline. There is a dichotomy at work here. True, the trend is your friend. But it is exactly that trend strength that gets these advisers to a bullish or bearish extreme.

Yet isn't the first rule of trading not to buck the trend?

I think the sentiment index helps us understand the old adage, "The trend is your friend . . . until the end."

The end of a trend, a moneymaking opportunity, comes when too many of these players have climbed aboard the bandwagon. In short, the sentiment data has as good a record of telling us when we are close to the end of the trend as anything I have seen in my 40 years of tracking stock prices.

Trend strength—that is, a strong rally—apparently has a hypnotic effect on market prognosticators. The greater the rally, the deeper their somnambulistic trance. Nothing gets these people more bullish than a rally. It is almost as though they stop thinking, and in lemminglike fashion, the closer to the end of a trend we are the greater the number wanting to jump off the cliff!

Should you take the time to study the index, you will see that near the end of the trend this camp is on the wrong side of the trade. They begin getting in phase with the trend around the midpoint, then become excessive in their view as the trend nears completion. In other words, the crowd can catch a trend and be correct, for a while. The stronger the trend the more committed to it these folks become.

Keep in mind that this group can and will be correct in their market outlook at the midpoint. It is when the crowd becomes extraordinarily one-sided, with readings above 75 percent as potential sells or below 25 percent as potential buys, that we are alerted to opportunity.

Our entire upbringing has been that the majority is right; they get to rule, they prevail. But the majority (or mob) rule can be a dangerous position. If there are three of us and two of us decide to kill you, should we have that right? The more I have seen the fallibility of the crowd the more I question how great the leaders we have voted into office really are! Since childhood we have been taught the majority is right. We decide the future based on a popular vote. If we are not certain, we take a survey!

The majority view is not always wrong; it is not a given it will be incorrect. But the evidence shows, and rather markedly so, the crowd is more likely to be wrong than right at the extremes. Thus we are given an advantage, a window of opportunity, when our odds for success are increased. What more could a speculator want?

Even then we should recognize that we might still be early, so we most likely need additional confirmation or a short-term entry technique to enter the trade. There are myriads of entry techniques, but without the proper setup, such as what the sentiment index provides, most are doomed to fail.

ADDITIONAL INSIGHT INTO THE INDEX

By now, I trust, you get the point—we have an index here of real value. And I suspect you have asked, is there any way we can filter out some of the less desirable calls it makes?

Certainly, there is, but don't expect to sidestep all the minefields, as that's never going to happen.

As a long-term buyer of a stock, I have noticed that the very best 25 percent buy signals come when the overall market trend is up. We can measure this in a most elementary way by simply saying that if the weekly closing price is above the 18-week moving average the longer-term trend is up.

If at this same time a sentiment index buy zone is reached it will be a better bet to buy than if the price is below the 18-week average of closing prices.

Let's begin the analysis with a weekly chart of Disney from 1997 into 2000 (see Figures 9.7 and 9.8). Here I have taken the liberty of marking with arrows the instances when both conditions were met—the long-term trend was positive (i.e., the weekly close of above the 18-week average was higher), while the sentiment index was below 25 percent. I have X'd out all the other signals. Notice how many of them there were! Some were good, some not so good; but all the signals when the two tools were in synch

DIS/Walt Disney Productions (1997–1999, weekly)

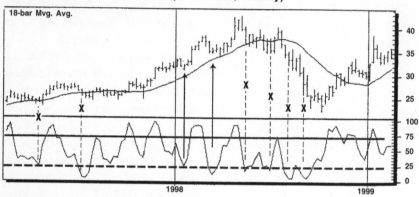

Figure 9.7   Disney 1997–1999

DIS/Walt Disney Productions (1998–2000, weekly)

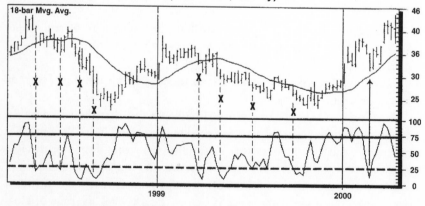

Figure 9.8   Disney 1998–2000

worked out. There were only three from 1997 into 2000. I like that; the fewer trades the better.

Keeping the preceding discussion in mind, let's revisit Merck in Figure 9.9, which shows only the buying indications when the two indicators were congruent. What a difference from Figure 9.3—far fewer trades, with virtually all of them making money if you exited the first time the index went above 75 percent.

DON'T INHALE

Figure 9.10, that of Philip Morris, presents plenty of opportunities to buy using the sentiment index. Many of them made money, until 1999 when class-action lawsuits brought prices tumbling. Note how none of the buy points would have been acted upon, because the weekly close was below the 18-week average.

There are certainly other approaches an investor might choose in order to filter out the less than ideal points, but this one is not bad.

Short selling would be instigated with just the opposite rules: the sentiment index above 75 percent while weekly closing prices are below the 18-bar average.

Finally, I am leaving you with seven charts to study of different stocks

MRK/Merck & Company Inc. (1996–2000, weekly)

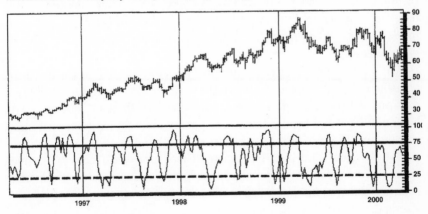

Figure 9.9   Merck 1996–2000

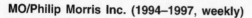

MO/Philip Morris Inc. (1994–1997, weekly)

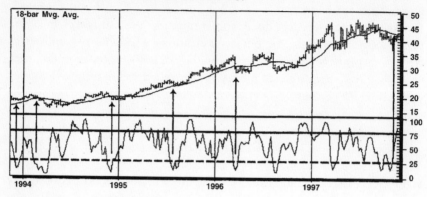

Figure 9.10   Philip Morris 1994–1997

and different time periods so you might get a better feel for the index and perhaps even develop your own way of using this valuable data. What I like best about this notion is that it is not paralogistic; it is the way markets have always worked since the early measurements of Garfield Drew.

WHY STOCKS DO WHAT THEY DO

In the long run stocks move up and down for real reasons—things like earnings, debt, insider buying, and the like. They really matter, as any long-term viewer of stock market history realizes. In fact, I believe these fundamentals to be among the best ways of isolating long-term position plays in equities.

However, on a shorter- or intermediate-term basis, prices fluctuate, and sometimes quite wildly. Many of these gyrations are undoubtedly random and defy prediction. Yet, the vast majority of these intermediate-term highs can be found to shape up at the precise moment my sentiment index is telling us there are too many buyers.

Market lows are just the reverse. The majority of them are formed when there are too many people thinking or advising others to sell, clear evidence that the market seems destined to prove the majority of people wrong the majority of the time.

An equally interesting point is that it does not seem to matter what the company does, or in the current market environment, doesn't do. What clearly does matter is that when too many of the crew get on one side of the stock market boat it's going to tip back the other way (unlike a real boat), just as when the majority think they have it figured out that the trend is up, its predestination is to change.

It will pay big dividends to study the fundamental underpinnings of a company to select long-term investments. But when it comes to timing the entry into these issues I certainly want to be doing what the majority of others are *not* doing.

Thanks to today's communications and Internet sites, it is possible to track and tabulate the mind-sets of many of the players in this game so that we, hopefully, do not get caught up in the peer pressures that make for market turning points.

NOTES FROM MY TRADING WITH THE INDEX

I have used this index in a variety of ways. The most interesting one is that I have written calls when the majority of the advisers are bullish. (One collects a premium from the buyer of the call, hence an immediate credit is given your account for the option price. You cannot make more than the premium paid to you, but you are certain of that profit. If, however, you are wrong, when you cover the position you can deduct from your loss the profit from the premium the call buyer paid you.) I've not done this often, but (knock on wood) so far I've never had a losing trade. My strategy has been to find a commodity (because that is what I primarily trade in), but the same idea has application and merit for stocks that are in substantial downtrends.

I do not want a trend to have been down for more than seven months, simply because we know that all trends, at some point, must end. There is a much higher probability for a seven- or eight-month trend to be reversed than one that has been in effect for just a couple of months.

Given that setup, a strong downtrend market, I then wait for the investor sentiment index to get above 80 percent. The week it does this, just before the close of Friday's business I write calls on the future contracts. Just to refresh your memory, writing a call gives someone the opportunity to buy the commodity (or it could be a stock) from me in the future. The bet the buyer of the call is making is that prices will go substantially higher, enough to pay off the premium I'm charging as well as to overcome the strike price (the price the call is written for). If I write a call on a stock at $36 a share to expire in 90 days, the call will be worthless if the price of the stock is equal to or less than $36 at expiration.

Since the advisers have been very bullish on the stock, or commodity, the option premium tends to be higher at these turning points due to the excessive optimism that prices will go higher. My objective in the trade has been a profit of 50 percent, so if the option that I've sold declines by more than 50 percent in value I nail down my profit. I do this procedure on Fridays because the poor patsy buying the option from me already faces two days of decaying premium. If the option were to go against me—that is, prices rally so much the option increases in premium to the point of being equal to the premium I was paid for the option—I would exit and scratch the trade.

The entire strategy is to find a nice downtrend market, wait until too many people get too bullish, then write call options. I've also done the reverse (write puts in an uptrend) with equal success.

Here I look for a market that is in a strong uptrend—but again, not one that's been in effect for more than seven months. I then write puts when the advisers get excessively bearish. My belief is that since the trend is up it will most likely continue and the advisers will again be incorrect. The nice thing about this type of option writing program is since the majority of advisers (and thus the public as well) are naive and pessimistic on the stock or futures contract and believe prices will go lower in the future, this makes them willing to pay more for a put option at this time as opposed to when the market has been rallying. This gives me the best of both worlds, a market set up to rally at a time people will pay even more than normal for a put option due to their emotional bearishness.

There are some stellar examples of how important this index can be in an investor's arsenal of timing tools, as you have seen. In addition to the prior examples, I'm showing a few more charts of individual stocks for your own study, notably Wal-Mart, Intel, and IBM. (See Figures 9.11 through 9.17.)

SEASONALITY AND STOCK PRICES

Commodity traders bring a unique perspective to the financial markets, as we have known for years that there are seasonal influences to commodity

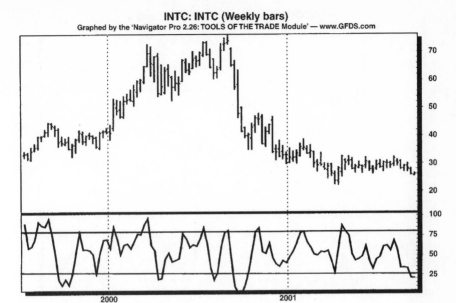

Figure 9.11 INTC

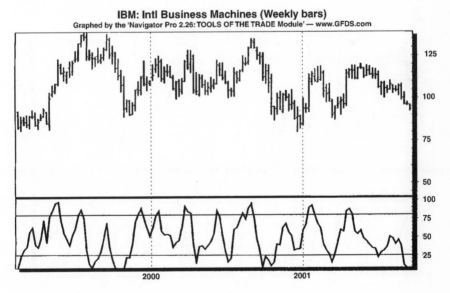

Figure 9.12 IBM

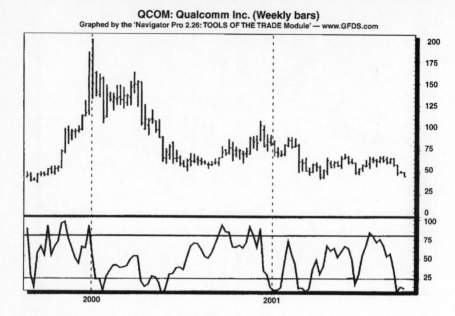

Figure 9.13   Qualcomm

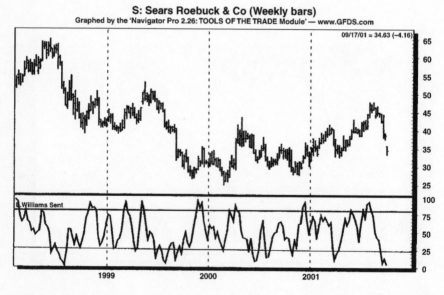

Figure 9.14   Sears

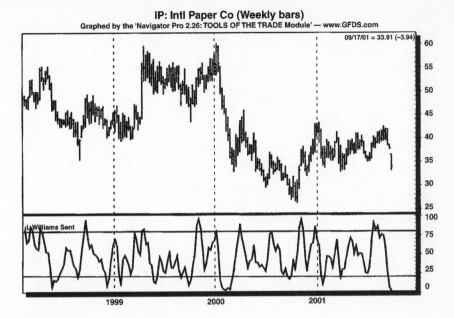

Figure 9.15 International Paper

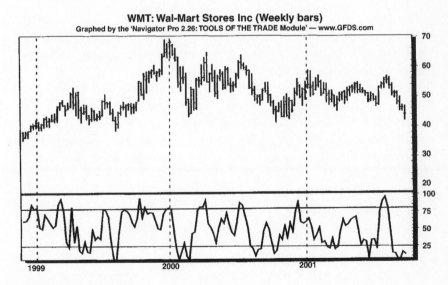

Figure 9.16 Wal-Mart

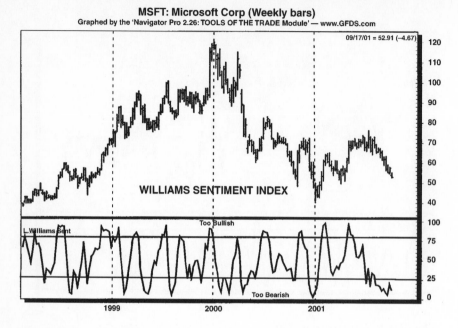

Figure 9.17   Microsoft

prices. As an example I would refer you to my book, *Sure Thing Commodity Trading: How Seasonal Factors Influence Commodity Prices*, written in 1973. The point of the book was that there are somewhat reliable seasonal times for commodities to rally or decline.

This may be more apparent in commodity prices due to weather and to harvest and planting time periods. Additionally, one can look at the consumption side of the equation; a simple example would be the egg market. Unfortunately, this market no longer trades, but when it did the price of eggs rallied, on a religious basis (no pun intended), just before Easter each year.

To the best of my knowledge I was the first to undertake a serious study of seasonal influences on stock prices. Yale Hirsch had done a little work on this in the 1960s, and I did an exhaustive study in the late 1970s covering more than 500 stocks to see if I could find times when some stocks have a reliable tendency to advance or decline.

The first stock I paid a great deal of attention to was IBM. I wrote, almost 20 years ago, "IBM is usually a buy around the last week of October with profits being taken toward the latter part of January. . . . Then look for a buy point in April and exits somewhere in the latter part of September." As Figure 9.18 shows, the seasonal tendency of IBM continues to this day.

Option writers can use this index as a general timing device of when to be writing calls at times suggested by seasonal market highs, and writing puts at times when we usually have seasonal low points. To pinpoint the precise time, whether you're buying or writing calls or puts, you can also bring into play the sentiment index so you get both in alignment. This is the ideal strategy for an investor, whether you do an out-and-out purchase or are fancy dancing in the option business.

Wal-Mart, the world's leading retailer, has a strong seasonal pattern of presenting a buying opportunity in February with most, though not all, market highs coming in mid to late July (see Figure 9.19). Sometimes this late July time marks a significant high, or at least a stopping point when the stock goes into a significant trading range with no upside progress being made for investors.

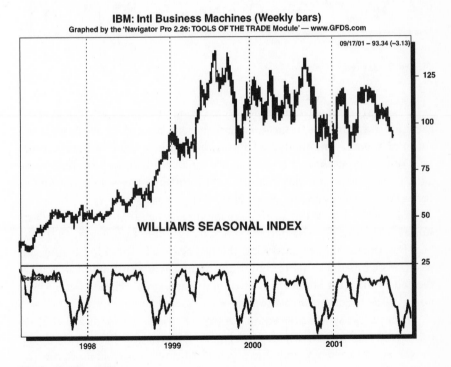

Figure 9.18   IBM

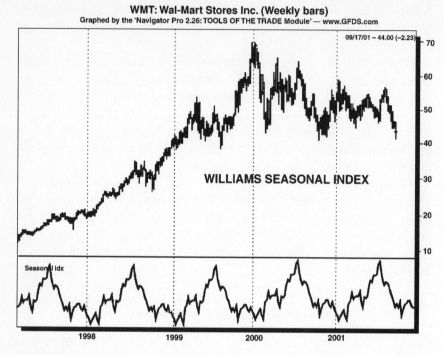

Figure 9.19   Wal-Mart

I have worked with this index long enough to gain a great deal of respect for it. It could be of great value to anyone who is accumulating a position in a stock. The road map is precise and clear; there are better times than others to purchase most issues. It would greatly behoove a fund manager, or you or me for that matter, to hold off purchases until the time is correct as evidenced by the seasonal tendency chart.

Coca-Cola has an interesting seasonal tendency that probably reflects summertime sales for this beverage. As you can note from Figure 9.20, the best buy time comes right around the last week of September or the first week of October. The more significant highs have been found to occur at the end of July, just about the time of maximum summertime sales, at least north of the equator, for this company.

Even stocks where one would not expect to see a seasonal tendency do exhibit strong repetitive patterns. Figure 9.21 of the Boeing Company shows the stock usually finds a low in mid-April with a sell close to the first week of August.

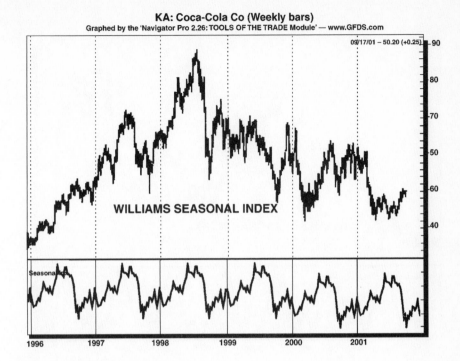

Figure 9.20 Coca-Cola

So that you might get a better understanding of the seasonal influences on individual stocks I have presented the seasonal tendencies of some of the most widely followed stocks for your perusal.

There is real value to these charts when they're used in combination with other indicators. As an example, the ideal sentiment sell signal would come at a time when the majority of investment advisors, 75 percent or more, are bullish while an individual stock at that same time is at the traditional seasonal high point of the stock. You're combining two indicators here, excess of optimism in conjunction with the seasonal pattern calling for a decline.

It is equally true for buy signals. Here we will be looking for a stock that is in the area of the traditional seasonal low, or buying area, and hope to find the investment advisory index excessively negative at this time. When we do see 75 percent or more of the newsletters writer saying "Don't buy this stock," we want to!

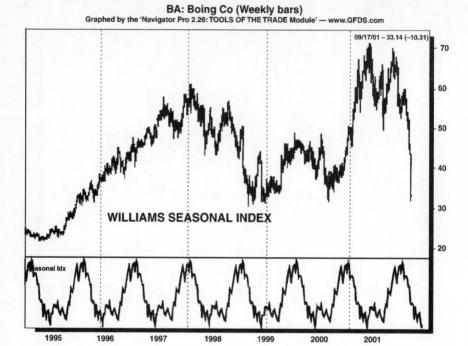

Figure 9.21   Boeing

The sentiment index is something I have created in conjunction with Genesis Financial Data Service. It is available from Genesis through its daily update service, or you may purchase the index on individual issues for your own personal databases or software configurations. Genesis can be reached at 1-800-808-3282 or at www.gfds.com. You can also obtain the sentiment index from Commodity Quote Graphics at www.CQG.com.

10

THE INVESTMENT CHALLENGE YOU FACE

To ridicule philosophy is to philosophize.
—Blaise Pascal

Most investors simply don't have a clue as to what the parameters of the game really are. The reason they come into the stock market is more to make a killing than it is to develop a consistent moneymaking machine. Not knowing what to expect means you don't have boundaries or the perspective of what is good and what is bad.

Let me tell you how good and bad stocks have been over the long pull. From 1926 forward, stocks have averaged 12.3 percent per year (1926–1993), while Treasury bills returned 3.74 percent per year on average. Long-term government bonds yielded 5.3 percent, and corporate bonds netted an investor 5.9 percent.

This needs to be placed in perspective, because while all showed gains, the clock was running. As inflation has averaged 3.2 percent per year, which knocks down the true rate of return. That's how much money you lost simply by holding onto cash. Inflation certainly takes its toll. In the case of the Treasury bill, investors' net gain was 0.54 percent over that 67-year time.

The bondholder did better but still not spectacularly well, while the true rate of return for the stockholder was 9.09 percent after inflation. This tells us what we should expect, on average, our investments to return. If you can do more than 9 percent per year, after inflation, you have beaten the markets.

The ancillary of this is why in the world people would incur debt with interest rates of 12 to 18 percent, a heavy tariff to pay, usually for the cost of holding onto a quickly depreciating luxury. These are two-time losers, losing not only the 9 percent a year they could get from stocks, but also interest rate payments of 12 to 18 percent. That means the alligator is biting them at a 21 to 27 percent rate! Now you see why no debt or very low debt is so incredibly important to an investor.

WHAT WE NEED TO DO

An investor has yet one more way to measure his or her investment success. The common yardstick is outperforming the broad-based market averages over the time period, which is usually the prior 12 months.

You would think this should not be so difficult, yet approximately 80 percent of the mutual funds do not beat the averages. This is highly significant because if you want to outperform normal performance, the odds of success are only 2 out of 10 if you turn your money over to a supposed expert in the business. Plus, the 20 percent who outperform the averages are not the same group every year! Only 20 percent of that 20 percent show consistency in beating the Dow Jones Industrial Average performance.

As I develop our master long-term strategy we will refer to this basis as a reference point in measuring our success, or lack thereof.

IT'S ALL ABOUT VALUE

By the time you are through reading this book you'll probably be sick and tired of hearing the word "value." But it is the most important concept an investor can use to gain an advantage in the game. Understand value and you will outperform not only the market but the vast majority of fund managers.

The idea of value has been around a surprisingly long time. This approach to investing most likely began with an article by Robert Weiss in 1930 ("Investing for True Value," *Barron's*, September 8, 1930) that culminated with this commentary: "The proper price of any security, whether a stock or a bond, is the sum of all the future income payments discounted at the current rate of interest in order to arrive at present value."

Samuel Elliott Gould added to the subject matter in 1931 with his article, "Stock Growth and Discount Tables" (Boston Financial Publishing). This author defined value as the average rate at which a company's earnings grow over time, the dividend that would have been paid over that same time, the price-earnings ratio, and finally the internal rate of return the investor needed to achieve.

If the pundits and advisers of the late 1990s had simply read and taken to heart these writings from the 1930s they would never have put a penny into the stocks that decimated their customers' long-term investments. So to that extent there are lessons from the past that do apply to our future.

The avowed father of fundamental analysis, Benjamin Graham, made an interesting comment in 1946: "In the years to come we analysts must go to school to learn the older established disciplines." Half a century later market soothsayers are still trying to develop new lessons and new rules on the assumption there is a new economy. There isn't. Obviously things change, and today's economy is not yesterday's economy. But value, like gravity, is always there regardless of what object we toss up in the air. Gravity doesn't care if it is new or old; it always exerts the same force.

And so it is with value, which is why so many nonvalue investors were hurt so much, and are always hurt when markets decline. Value is the core of all investment success, while trend is the basis of all profits. Trend is a direct result of fundamental considerations—that is, value.

While investors are lured by the possibility of gargantuan returns, it goes without saying that the greater the potential reward, the greater the risk.

Speculating is about maximizing your return in the shortest time. That is not what investing is about; investing is about consistently making more than the guy next to you.

In my case I am more than willing to let the guy next to me make a killing every now and then because I know in the long run, since he is assuming undue risk, those rewards will have their setbacks along the way. This means on average I will outperform someone who does not have a strategy or program to approach the markets.

One needs to find the balance between risk and ample rewards. If your main goal in life is to escape worry, you will stay poor. Tranquility has advantages, but it doesn't bring about monetary wealth. Given a choice between being worried and being poor, I'll take worry every time. As Sigmund Freud replied, when asked about how to achieve a state of balance, "And for what? Balance can only achieve the happiness of quietness."

Risk is a funny thing in that you have absolutely no hope of becoming wealthy in the stock market without taking on risk. But this is a two-edged sword, because that same risk can cause you to lose your wealth. Thus risk control becomes our key ingredient in long-term investment success. Risk creates and destroys wealth.

THE ONLY THREE WAYS TO CONTROL RISK

I have done a great deal of research and have concluded there are only three ways one can control risk while still retaining the potential for gain. The three considerations, or factors, that influence our exposure to risk are:

1. The quality of the investment one makes.
2. When you decide to purchase the investment.
3. How much of your bankroll goes into that investment.

Obviously, the lower quality the investment is, the greater your risk will become. Invest with low-quality people and expect low-quality results. Invest in junk and you're going to get junk back. This chapter will be focused on determining what is and what is not "junk" in the stock market.

The time when you decide to make a purchase is just as important as the quality. If you bought Microsoft at the right time you would have made a fortune. So timing makes a difference. Never let anyone tell you otherwise.

The problem with finding quality and selecting the right time is that doing so does have its subtle nuances. We can codify this to an extent, even developing rules and strategies, yet there is part science and part art to this. In other words, judgment will be involved, but isn't judgment involved every day in our lives and in everything that we do? Of course it is, but given a sound foundation, your judgment will serve you better than a person without a good understanding of the subject matter at hand.

Finally, the amount of money you plunk down into your investment determines your exposure to potential risk. Had you bought one share of

Microsoft, even at the high, you may well have been able to endure the pain of its decline. But had you put in your entire life savings it would be a totally different story. That's why the entire Chapter 12 is devoted to money management—so you can determine what percentage of your portfolio, or life savings, should go into any particular investment. This makes certain you control risk, that you are the driving force of risk, as opposed to risk being the driving force of your life.

All this is very good news: An investor can control risk. Speculators and plungers seemingly seek to expand risk in hopes of higher returns, yet the risk ultimately pulls down even their most spectacular gains.

SEVEN TRADITIONAL MEASURES OF VALUE

Analysts have conventionally used seven ways to measure the fundamental aspect of a stock and its potential future returns

1. *Price-to Earnings Ratio*—The most widely known measure of value is the price-to-earnings ratio, which is arrived at by dividing the current price of the stock by current earnings. The higher this number is, the more investors are paying for what the company is earning. A high P/E number therefore suggests difficulty in further advance of price. Traditionally, analysts have said the lower the P/E ratio is, the more positive future market activity should be.

2. *Price-to-Book Ratio*—Price-to-book ratio is arrived at by dividing the current price of your stock by the book value per share. The notion is that a low value would indicate an investor is paying close to the liquidating value of the assets of the company. The lower the ratio is, the more bullish should be the future prospects of your stock.

3. *Price-to-Cash Flow Ratio*—The next common way of looking at the value of an issue would be what is known as the price-to-cash flow ratio. This ratio is obtained by simply dividing the market value of the stock by the cash flow of the company. Analysts who prefer this approach point out that earnings can be manipulated by accounting techniques and crafty green-shaded gnomes, while it is much more difficult to obscure total cash flow. What one looks for here is again a low value on the assumption that therefore the stock should perform better in the future.

4. *Price-to-Sales Ratio*—A relatively new innovation in measuring value has been the price-to-sales ratio. It is similar to the price-to-earnings ratio but compares the price of a stock to the total annual sales instead of earnings. High price-to-sales ratios are typically bearish, low ones bullish.

5. *Yield*—Dividend yields are yet one more measure of value. Here the question is what return an investor gets from directly holding the stock. There is always the potential for market appreciation, but what about the dividend the company pays? The theory is that high-dividend stocks are good values. The mere fact the company can pay a dividend tells us it is making money and gives us the best of both worlds, potential upside appreciation coupled with a return on our investment.

6. *Return on Equity*—Return on equity is a value marker that has been used for many years. It is arrived at by dividing the equity of the stock into income (after all expenses excluding dividends). This number is multiplied by 100 to place it in a percentage basis. Here, the higher the number the better.

7. *Relative Strength*—The last measure that is widely used by funds and money managers received its notoriety in the 1960s when many analysts said the relative price performance of an issue compared to another issue had predictive value. This is called relative strength and usually looks at the price change of all stocks today versus where they were 12 months ago. By and large it is assumed that stocks with high relative strength numbers, the ones that have been going up, will continue going up.

Now let's turn our attention to these values. Each has merit in helping us select stocks that have the highest probability for upside appreciation. The more you understand these techniques, the better you should be able to implement them in your own investment decisions.

MORE ON DETERMINING VALUE

In 1969 Paul Miller, while at Drexel & Co., did a fascinating study of the Dow Jones Industrial Average stocks by dividing the index into two groups. Miller first took the 10 stocks in the Dow with the highest P/E ratios and studied their rates of return from 1937 to 1969. He compared them with the 10 stocks in the Dow with the lowest P/E ratios. Finally, as a balance against all this, he looked at the total return on all 30 Dow Jones Industrial Average stocks.

The results are actually staggering. While Miller broke the study down into four-year increments, I'm listing here just the total results of that 32-year period. But let me point out that in each four-year increment the 10 lowest P/E stocks did better than the 10 highest P/E issues or the average itself. Talk about an advantage in the game!

Dow's 1937–1969 Stock Performance

10 lowest P/E stocks	11.7%
10 highest P/E stocks	2.3%
All 30 Dow stocks	6.6%

If you have ever wondered whether quality matters, whether some stocks are just naturally better than others, the preceding list makes it perfectly clear, beyond any reasonable doubt: Stocks with low price-to-earnings ratios do better than high price-to-earnings stocks. In this case the low P/E stocks outperformed the high ones by 500 percent and almost doubled the return on the average Dow stock.

Another study, this one by David Dreman in 1979, looked at stocks from 1968 to 1977 and the returns of high P/E versus low P/E stocks over time periods of six months, one year, and three years. The basis of comparison was the average of all stocks, which gained 4.75 percent in the nine-year study.

His study revealed the highest P/E stocks, bought and held for three years, on average lost 1.4 percent.

The lowest P/E stocks, bought and held for three years, gained 10.89 percent.

Here's the bottom-line truth of investing: Low P/E stocks outperform high P/E stocks. This has been proven—and reproven—over a wide variety of time periods, markets, and companies of all sorts of different makeups. This is the underlying reality of the marketplace. It is how one finds value, locates quality, and eliminates, or least moderates, risk exposure.

Additional Research

A study presented by John Slatter in his book, *Safe Investing: How to Make Money without Losing Your Shirt* (Books Britain, 1991), assumed buying the 10 highest-yielding Dow Jones Industrial Average stocks every January, then the following January replacing the lower-yielding ones with stocks that had higher yields than those in the original portfolio.

The results are quite impressive for this approach. Had one begun doing this program 30 years ago, by the time 1990 rolled around a $10,000 investment would have been worth more than $800,000. Investors who simply purchased the Dow and held on would have seen their $10,000 grow to slightly over $200,000. Get the message? High-yield stocks outperform the average stock by a factor of four.

Slatter also showed that during bear markets the high-yield portfolio substantially outperformed the averages themselves. On average, Dow stocks lost 15.5 percent during bear market slides while the 10 high-yielding Dow stocks on average lost only 3.3 percent. Talk about controlling risk. By buying high-yield stocks one would have been able to have reduced risk by a factor of five on the downside while increasing the return by a factor of four on the upside.

Jeremy Siegel, writing in *Stocks for the Long Run* (McGraw-Hill, 2002), presents similar data on buying the 10 Dow stocks with the highest yields versus buying the Dow Jones Industrial Average itself from 1928 to 1997, and has broken the return down into various time periods.

Any way you slice it, high-yield stocks outperform the average itself over a long time. The total results from 1928 to 1997 show a gain of 13.2 percent for the high-yield stocks and 11.4 percent for the Dow itself (keep in mind these 10 high-yield stocks are in the total Dow performance, so if we took them out the 11.4 percent would be reduced substantially), while the S&P 500 gained 10.64 percent.

The only time the high-yield stocks did not outperform the Dow itself was in the 1930s—the Depression. But both before and after the Depression the high-yield Dow stocks have always outperformed the averages. Perhaps most noteworthy is the 1973–1974 bear market during which the Dow itself was off about 26 percent and the S&P 500 down close to 40 percent. These were proving grounds for a system or strategy, and quality had its reward in spades. The amazing strength and wisdom of selecting quality and value were shown by the 10 high-yield Dow stocks; they posted a *gain* of about 3 percent. Granted, not much of a gain, but compared to a loss of 30 percent, I'll take that measly 3 percent any year.

In James P. O'Shaughnessy's book, *What Works on Wall Street* (McGraw-Hill, 1998), each of the ratios is dissected and its impact on stocks revealed for the first time. This monumental study is very significant, making for a book that is a must-have and must-read. I will summarize the results, but you need to read the entire book. O'Shaughnessy shows the impact of these value ratings and calculates the results of these gauges on different groups of stocks. I have chosen to show them only on large issues as I believe those stocks are more stable, hence offer us less risk and downside exposure.

The results reflect a $10,000 investment from 1951 to 1996.

	Result	*Annual Gain*
Price-to-earnings ratio	$3,787,460	14.10%
Price-to-book ratio	$5,490,121	15.05%
Price-to-cash flow	$5,773,333	15.18%
Price-to-sales ratio	$3,853,418	14.15%
High dividend yield	$2,898,099	13.43%
Return on equity	$1,138,300	11.10%
Relative strength	$4,429,185	14.50%

The first point to make is that while there is a large difference between which technique you use and the investment results to attain, each valuation measure exceeded what stocks did on average during that same time. It is good news that in an absolute fashion we have found some things that help us beat the averages.

The question now becomes, how can one best use these techniques? The O'Shaughnessy study went just a little bit further in the analysis of earnings per share that I would like to touch on. He did one study looking at large stocks that had the biggest one-year earnings increases and noted those stocks actually underperformed the market averages. The hypothetical $10,000 grew to $1,292,138; that makes for an 11.68 percent annualized gain. He then looked at the same stocks but checked out the results of those that had the largest five-year increases in earnings per share.

This is what the long-term buy-and-hold crowd thinks works—that these stocks should outperform the market. O'Shaughnessy's work suggests otherwise. The $10,000 investment in large stocks with the highest five-year compound earnings didn't do very well. At the end of the time it would have been worth $613,441 for an annual return of 10.3 percent. So much for long-term rate of earnings increases.

METHOD TO THE MADNESS OF WALL STREET

What we see here is that there is rhyme and reason to the way Wall Street works. It takes no rocket scientist to figure out that if you buy value stocks, at any given point in time, and hold onto them you will do better than simply buying the averages themselves. Since our goal as long-range investors is to outperform the averages we can now attain that with a high degree of confidence. Our goal is easily within our reach.

If we decide to try to significantly outperform the market by selecting one or two hot stocks, we now know we can statistically increase our chances of being correct if we stay with stocks that have positive fundamental readings. As brokers and investment advisers sing their songs to sway us to part with our hard-earned cash we can simply compare notes to see whether those stocks fit our criteria.

The most significant negative, as O'Shaughnessy sees it, is definitely that of an extreme price-to-sales reading. Work I have done, as well as work done by others, indicates it is far safer to buy a stock that has a 1.0 or lower price-to-sales reading if you want to ensure your chances against failure.

If you were to couple that with requiring your stock to have a low price-to-book ratio or cash flow ratio, I think you are virtually assured of outperforming the market averages using the last two readings. If you want to look for the "discount to earnings" selection technique I've presented here you could assure yourself of a better opportunity by again referring to this fundamental knowledge or wisdom.

The main thing I want to steer you away from is buying rumor or concept stocks. We know stocks go up for only one of two reasons: hype and hope or value and value. The hype and hope stocks may well have exponential rises. They can show spectacular performance, but the problem is that they crash in an equally spectacular fashion. Indeed, the stocks are subject to spectacular declines. That is part and parcel of investing in stocks that do not have underlying value. Why place ourselves and our money at risk in such a scenario? It is beyond me that reasonably intelligent people make such unintelligent investment decisions.

But greed . . . what an emotion . . . a brief phone call, a few words about how great things will be in the future and how much the stock has already rallied, and the human mind simply blows out all logical circuits. That voice inside your head is saying, "There's quick and easy money to be made here, and that money is mine," while what you should be doing is checking the underlying conditions. It amazes me that people will spend months looking for the best car in order to buy one that fits their needs and represents the best value, but will make an investment decision on 10 times that amount of money in just a few seconds!

There is always plenty of time to invest. Anytime anyone, about any stock, says you have to get in today, right now, warning flags should go up. There's always a place to get into the market. Time is our friend, not our enemy. Let's make no rush to judgments when it comes to investing.

11

PUTTING IT ALL TOGETHER FOR LONG-TERM INVESTMENT SUCCESS

*It's not who you know, but what you know . . .
and now you will know!*

By now you realize that it does make a difference *when* you buy and sell stocks and also *which ones* you buy and sell. By now you understand there is reality to the marketplace; that certain things matter. Those things are primarily earnings but they also include the buying and selling your of stock by mutual funds or insiders.

As described in the preceding chapter, James P. O'Shaughnessy turned his computers on for a study of things such as price-to-earnings ratios, price-to-book ratios, price-to-cash flow ratios, the value of dividend yields, and relative strength or momentum. Those of you who have studied his work know he places the most importance on price-to-sales ratios and momentum along with companies with smaller capitalizations.

While I think the world of the work this gentleman has done, I differ with him on two of these supposed indicators. The first is that of market capitalization. O'Shaughnessy looked at the returns of stocks with market capitalization by breaking them down into zones of those companies with less than $25 million, $25 million to $100 million, $100 million to $250 million, then stepping up to $500 million, up to $1 billion, and finally those companies with over $1 billion of capitalization.

O'Shaughnessy concluded that "stocks with market capitalizations between $25,000 and $100 million, as well as those with market capital-izations between $100,000 and $250 million, do outperform large stocks on an absolute basis, but fail when risk is taken into account."

This suggests to me that there may not be a distinct advantage to this particular group of stocks. Most prognosticators, though, have seen this the other way around and have focused their attention on small-cap stocks. I believe that to be in error, and here's why.

There further appears to be a distinct advantage in this game of selecting stocks with capitalization *under* $25 million. No doubt about it; this group of stocks substantially outperformed the other cap groups. O'Shaughnessy's work shows that $10,000 invested in these types of stocks in 1951 would have grown to $800,000 by 1966. Many advi-sory services and funds grabbed onto this little tidbit of information from O'Shaughnessy and became very big advocates of buying low-cap companies.

There is a distinct problem with this approach, however. It is simply this: The small companies in this study, and to the best of my knowledge in all studies of this kind, have a distinct bias to them. The bias is that there were many, many small-cap companies that never made it through all the years. They went bankrupt, or bust, someplace along the way. Thus the losers are not in the database. All one finds in the database are the winners! That simple little fact of life, I believe, severely skews any re-ports on the value of investing in small issues. So, the next time you get the song and dance about investing in small caps you might want to think of this bias.

Additionally, as O'Shaughnessy points out, it is extremely difficult to be invested in the stocks, simply because there's such little trading volume in them.

Figure 11.1 reflects the results of small-cap funds and the S&P 500 from 1991 into 2001. As the graph shows, small caps substantially under-performed the market from 1998 into 2001, when both small caps and the S&P came into synch with each other. The actual performance of these issues indicates there is little if any advantage to small-cap stocks. True, they certainly did outperform the market averages from 1991 into 1998, but following that point the broad-based S&P 500 outperformed the small caps.

So while many analysts have indicated small-cap funds should and will outperform the market averages, that has not been the case in reality. What's more important, I believe, is the inherent bias of their research

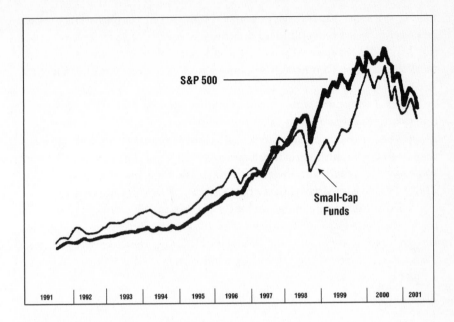

Figure 11.1   S&P 500 versus Small-Cap Funds

with the dropout effect of so many small-cap companies that are no longer in existence.

Another point of contention I have, not so much with O'Shaughnessy but with followers of his work, is their love of his data that shows stocks with the best relative strength tend to have the best future performance. This is the old adage of what goes up should continue going up. But the reality is that may not last for long. His best portfolio strategy is that of buying stocks with high relative strength. The problem, however, is that the risk one is exposed to with these stocks is substantially greater than with stocks selected on fundamental criteria alone. It is for this reason that I would prefer to focus strictly on the underlying conditions that cause price, rather than price itself.

It's just like Logic 101 in college, when you were told you cannot predict A with A—which is exactly what technicians and market mathematicians have done for years. They simply looked at the trend of price to predict the future trend of price. Such an approach is destined to have you buying stocks at a major high at some point. It's like my Russian roulette analogy; there's a bullet in there for you.

My goal as an investor is consistent rates of return greater than the market averages. That brings me contentment. To achieve it I need to control risk.

Thus, I think it is wise that we let someone else take the risk. I really don't care if others make a killing in the market or outperform me at any given time. I say that because I absolutely know that on a longer-term basis they won't beat my consistent program. No way! They may well have some big up years, but they will also have some horrible down years. Those down years wipe away all the champagne bubbles of the past.

If I want to speculate on catching a big winner, all I need to do is refer to the technique of buying stocks at a "discount" in relation to earnings growth. There are plenty of opportunities using this technique to find stocks destined for strong up moves while at the same time being invested in quality.

WHEN A MARKET LOW COMES

At some point in the not too distant future, stocks will be under pressure, declining. Most investors will be on the sidelines or licking their wounds from the beating they have been taking. That's exactly the scenario where you want to begin looking for investment opportunities. You might refer to the investment advisory or any of the other sentiment data to suggest a market low is close at hand.

At that time you can begin poring through chart books, data from your broker, or advisory services such as *Value Line* or *Investor's Business Daily* to ferret out stocks that have continued to have increases in earnings yet have declined in price for the current quarter. Almost any brokerage firm can give you the earnings estimate so you'll know coming into the end of that quarter whether the relationship or a diversion does exist.

The key ingredient to the O'Shaughnessy study, I believe, is his study of future price activity in relation to what he has identified as the price-to-sales ratio. This is similar to the price-to-earnings ratio. However, it is not a reflection of earnings, but rather that of sales to the number of shares outstanding times price. This is arrived at by taking the total capitalization of the company and dividing this by annual sales. All we're looking at here is revenues to shares as opposed to earnings to shares.

There is an apparent problem here; the company may have large revenues but no profits. That's a distinct possibility. O'Shaughnessy has described this ratio as the "King of the Value Factors." In one of his studies he took the 50 lowest price-to-sales ratio stocks (the bullish ones) and compared those to the 50 highest price-to-sales ratio issues. He calculated that $10,000 invested in this group of stocks in 1951 would have turned into $8.2 million dollars by 1996. That's a 16 percent per year compounded rate of return.

Had an investor chosen to invest that same $10,000 in the 50 stocks with the highest price-to-sales ratios in 1951, the $10,000 would have been worth $91,000 in 1996. What a huge and gargantuan difference this price-to-sales ratio can make.

If you want to control the risk of your investments then you'd definitely want to pay attention to this price-to-sales ratio. I performed an interesting study of my own, thanks to the folks at Qualitative Analytics in Chicago (312-322-4690). In my study we looked at buying the Dow Jones Industrial Average too each year at the end of October. Our selection criteria as to which stocks to purchase was broken down in four ways.

In one test we bought the five Dow stocks with the highest price-to-sales ratios, in the next the five stocks with the lowest price-to-sales ratios in the Dow. We then turned our attention to the five stocks with the highest P/E ratios, and completed the test by looking at the five stocks with the lowest P/E ratios.

The results are fascinating:

Selection Technique	Annual Return 1980–2000
High price-to-sales	10.74%
Low price-to-sales	15.74%
High price-to-earning	14.69%
Low price-to-earnings	15.98%
Low yield	11.13%
High yield	15.95%
Low price and high yield	20.08%

This is staggering! An investor who had the wisdom to place money in the five Dow stocks with the lowest price-to-sales or lowest P/E ratio stocks made almost 16 percent per year. An investor purchasing the high

P/E stocks didn't do quite as well, and the value buyer did better but only by a percentage point.

However, the investor in the high price-to-sales stocks blew an opportunity for profits. The value-seeking investors earned 5 percent more per year, on average. The 5 percent a year is staggering when you begin to compound this performance.

The lesson should be perfectly clear—to avoid risk. Avoid stocks with high price-to-sales ratios. An operating rule based on my study would be that you do not want to buy stocks with a price-to-sales ratio in excess of 1.0. The lower the better. Given a choice between two stocks, both of which fit our fundamental criteria and one with a price-to-sales ratio of .95 and the other .65, it's an easy choice. Take the one at .65.

Interestingly enough, we did this same study on the Dow Jones Utility Average to see what effect, if any, the same filters might have on performance in this interest rate sensitive average. My idea here was to purchase the utilities starting the first week of April and exiting the first week of October. There has been a distinct seasonal tendency for the Utility Average to rally at this particular time, which is the reason the study focused in on just this zone of opportunity.

Let's take a look now at the performance breakdown based on the same fundamental considerations we just used in the Dow Jones Industrial Average.

Selection Technique	Annual Return 1980–2000
High price-to-sales	8.89%
Low price-to-sales	9.77%
High price-to-earnings	6.90%
Low price-to-earnings	10.43%
Low yield	10.36%
High yield	10.33%
Low price and high yield	11.82%

Again we see the importance of these ratios. While the utilities were not quite as responsive to the high price-to-sales ratio, there still is a substantial difference, almost three percentage points per year, between the worst approach and the best approach. What is consistent is that high P/E and high price-to-share studies show this is not as productive as doing it the other way around.

Notice that in both the Dow Jones Industrial and Dow Jones Utility studies the most profitable (highest-yielding,) return came from purchasing the lowest priced stocks with the highest yield. This, then, is the ultimate combination for investment success. There are two reasons why adding the low price criterion improves performance. The first is simply one of mathematics. It is easier for a $10 stock to have a 10 percent gain than for a $100 stock to have 10 percent gain.

That may explain the second reason going on here, which is that investors, funds, and such are more attracted to the lower-price stocks. Perhaps they, too, note it easier for them to have a larger percentage gain—that it should come quicker and easier than for a high-priced stock. What do bargain hunters look for? Not high-priced stocks. They look for low-priced stocks. That's why this combination of low price and high yield comes out ahead.

I'd now like to open up my private files to you on research I've done along this line on a whole host of fundamental measures. Much of this you may have read about, or will, and will hear many voices claiming many things about the importance of these ratios. Well, here, I think for the first time ever, are the answers to these ratios. Here is ratio reality.

The following studies are focused on just the Dow 30 stocks. As you will see I have tested a variety of ratios and sometimes used these ratios on the five highest-priced or five lowest-priced stocks in the Dow 30. Each test represents a hypothetical buy in mid-October along with an exit on April 15 or the last trading day in the following August. (Apr15Pct = % change from October to April; AugLTDPct = % change from October to August.) This gives you the opportunity to see what effect time has on a value measure. The last two columns are the most relevant as they reflect the percent of gain or loss in the time period.

The first test is our standard to measure valuation performances against. Table 11.1 reflects buying all 30 of the Dow Jones Industrial Average stocks with the entry and exit dates per the preceding paragraph. The average October-to-April gain has been 5.5 percent from 1975 through 2001. Had you bought all 30 of the Dow stocks and exited in April, that's what you would have earned. Now, you and I would like to do better. Maybe we can, but we need to compare other selection techniques against this performance to see whether we can select stocks more apt to advance. If we beat this performance yardstick, we have beaten the market.

Table 11.1 All Dow Jones Industrial Average Portfolio

Date	Port	Apr15Amnt	AugLTDAmnt	Apr15Pct	AugLTDPct
10/27/1975	DJ_ALL_PORT	0.986	18.487	1.066	19.977
10/29/1976	DJ_ALL_PORT	0.019	0.301	−0.478	−7.474
10/31/1977	DJ_ALL_PORT	−0.026	−0.460	0.839	15.028
10/30/1978	DJ_ALL_PORT	0.805	13.482	0.992	16.616
10/29/1979	DJ_ALL_PORT	−0.179	−2.854	1.279	20.401
10/27/1980	DJ_ALL_PORT	0.903	12.239	−0.034	−0.465
10/26/1981	DJ_ALL_PORT	0.330	4.799	1.282	18.616
10/29/1982	DJ_ALL_PORT	2.450	27.138	3.330	36.895
10/31/1983	DJ_ALL_PORT	−0.797	−6.264	0.340	2.673
10/29/1984	DJ_ALL_PORT	1.476	11.542	2.009	15.708
10/28/1985	DJ_ALL_PORT	4.566	31.969	5.096	35.682
10/27/1986	DJ_ALL_PORT	4.863	25.533	9.507	49.913
10/26/1987	DJ_ALL_PORT	3.378	17.688	3.890	20.368
10/31/1988	DJ_ALL_PORT	2.415	9.928	7.248	29.799
10/30/1989	DJ_ALL_PORT	1.756	5.851	−0.304	−1.014
10/29/1990	DJ_ALL_PORT	7.681	28.019	10.854	39.595
10/28/1991	DJ_ALL_PORT	5.346	13.932	3.907	10.182
10/26/1992	DJ_ALL_PORT	3.760	8.816	7.561	17.730
10/29/1993	DJ_ALL_PORT	−0.011	−0.021	4.051	7.994
10/31/1994	DJ_ALL_PORT	6.416	11.668	12.985	23.613
10/30/1995	DJ_ALL_PORT	13.897	19.735	15.135	21.493
10/28/1996	DJ_ALL_PORT	10.659	11.783	27.032	29.881
10/27/1997	DJ_ALL_PORT	35.171	32.391	11.205	10.319
10/26/1998	DJ_ALL_PORT	31.389	23.436	31.768	23.719
10/29/1999	DJ_ALL_PORT	−7.319	−4.401	1.028	0.618
10/30/2000	DJ_ALL_PORT	−6.703	−4.090	−5.513	−3.364
10/29/2001	DJ_ALL_PORT	17.838	12.187	−7.893	−5.392

5.5% Average Gain

Largest Increase in Profit Margin

Let's start with a test of what takes the October buy in the five Dow stocks that had the largest increase in profit margins over the past 12 months (see Table 11.2).

Numerous authors contend this is the best possible value measure for selecting a stock. What we see here is that since 1975 such a selection tech-

Table 11.2 Five Largest 12-Month Increases in Profit Margin in Dow Jones
Industrial Average

Date	Port	Apr15Amnt	AugLTDAmnt	Apr15Pct	AugLTDPct
10/27/1975	DJProfit_PORT	2.164	1.538	24.998	17.762
10/29/1976	DJProfit_PORT	1.061	0.752	10.659	7.552
10/31/1977	DJProfit_PORT	−0.392	0.384	−3.841	3.757
10/30/1978	DJProfit_PORT	1.297	2.553	12.611	24.819
10/29/1979	DJProfit_PORT	−0.777	2.276	−6.893	20.193
10/27/1980	DJProfit_PORT	−0.764	−2.593	−5.860	−19.892
10/26/1981	DJProfit_PORT	0.419	1.500	4.615	16.513
10/29/1982	DJProfit_PORT	2.212	3.308	19.444	29.073
10/31/1983	DJProfit_PORT	−2.647	−0.494	−18.148	−3.387
10/29/1984	DJProfit_PORT	1.335	1.687	9.889	12.499
10/28/1985	DJProfit_PORT	4.597	0.224	33.634	1.641
10/27/1986	DJProfit_PORT	1.745	4.274	13.494	33.052
10/26/1987	DJProfit_PORT	2.821	3.443	26.445	32.274
10/31/1988	DJProfit_PORT	0.718	5.014	4.770	33.288
10/30/1989	DJProfit_PORT	0.539	−1.346	2.785	−6.946
10/29/1990	DJProfit_PORT	3.953	6.353	23.733	38.147
10/28/1991	DJProfit_PORT	0.891	0.845	3.929	3.723
10/26/1992	DJProfit_PORT	4.610	8.405	20.110	36.665
10/29/1993	DJProfit_PORT	−4.030	−3.215	−12.843	−10.247
10/31/1994	DJProfit_PORT	2.115	7.062	7.617	25.430
10/30/1995	DJProfit_PORT	8.412	5.259	23.234	14.526
10/28/1996	DJProfit_PORT	1.527	11.015	3.552	25.619
10/27/1997	DJProfit_PORT	13.176	1.290	27.991	2.741
10/26/1998	DJProfit_PORT	13.227	17.730	23.514	31.519
10/29/1999	DJProfit_PORT	−12.760	−9.845	−18.202	−14.044
10/30/2000	DJProfit_PORT	−0.624	−2.528	−0.974	3.944
10/29/2001	DJProfit_PORT	5.601	−1.870	9.800	−3.271
					8.9% Average Gain

nique has had good and bad years with an average rate of return of 8.9
percent per "year" (keep in mind this is a six-month hold, as we are exiting
in April). Of 27 years all but seven made money, so it won 74 percent of
the time. More importantly, we beat the market, making a rate of return
62 percent greater than the 5.5 percent benchmark.

Net Working Capital

Table 11.3 reflects the same timing strategy, this time applied to the five stocks with the highest net working capital as well as the five with the lowest. One theory of the stock market is that working capital is king. The more money you have to work with the better, plus it tends to indicate a well-run company.

Fascinating information here: The highest net working capital companies averaged 9.2 percent for the six months and made money in 81 percent of the 27 years. The lowest net working capital companies actually did better, by quite a bit, netting 13.9 percent, on average. Accuracy dropped to 21 winning years or 77 percent correct. These simple values measure a way to outperform the market with a gain 3.2 times greater than the market, on average. In the fund I manage I use this type of approach with some weighting factors.

Price Matters

Now I'd like to show you what happens when we use these same criteria against the price of the stocks as a filter. Table 11.4 shows the results for buying the five highest-priced stocks in the Dow with the highest net working capital ratio. The second tabulation is that of the five lowest-priced stocks with the lowest net working capital ratio. There is quite a difference here, and it is one you will see across all these values. It is that lower-priced stocks outperform their higher-priced counterparts. There is some logic to this; bargain hunters like low prices, and it's easier for a $30 stock to rally 3 points for a 10 percent gain than a $200 stock to rally 20 points for that same 10 percent return.

The high-priced issues netted 10.9 percent while the low-priced ones brought in 11.7 percent. Also check out the accuracy: In the 27-year study six years lost money in the higher-priced issues while only three years lost in the lower-priced stocks.

THE TRUTH ABOUT YIELD, CASH FLOW, PRICE-TO-SALES, AND A WHOLE LOT MORE

You have your work cut out for you with Tables 11.5 and 11.6. I am presenting here my studies. Again keep in mind the buy and hold periods for a

Table 11.3 Highest and Lowest Net Working Capital in Dow Jones
Industrial Average

| | | Five Highest Net Working Capital | | | |
Date	Port	Apr15 Amnt	AugLTD Amnt	Apr15 Pct	AugLTD Pct
10/27/1975	DJWCAPHI_PORT	1.176	1.302	15.413	17.072
10/29/1976	DJWCAPHI_PORT	−0.218	−0.332	−2.404	−3.657
10/31/1977	DJWCAPHI_PORT	−0.209	0.120	−2.464	1.423
10/30/1978	DJWCAPHI_PORT	0.560	1.388	6.883	17.075
10/29/1979	DJWCAPHI_PORT	−0.551	1.308	−6.136	14.551
10/27/1980	DJWCAPHI_PORT	0.319	−0.177	3.153	−1.754
10/26/1981	DJWCAPHI_PORT	0.329	1.051	3.648	11.665
10/29/1982	DJWCAPHI_PORT	1.935	3.392	17.455	30.600
10/31/1983	DJWCAPHI_PORT	0.131	1.574	0.904	10.843
10/29/1984	DJWCAPHI_PORT	1.422	1.824	9.126	11.700
10/28/1985	DJWCAPHI_PORT	4.621	4.970	26.508	28.508
10/27/1986	DJWCAPHI_PORT	5.463	10.938	25.289	50.631
10/26/1987	DJWCAPHI_PORT	1.922	1.912	8.652	8.610
10/31/1988	DJWCAPHI_PORT	2.710	8.334	10.152	31.225
10/30/1989	DJWCAPHI_PORT	1.372	−1.540	4.086	−4.586
10/29/1990	DJWCAPHI_PORT	2.953	3.163	9.441	10.111
10/28/1991	DJWCAPHI_PORT	2.208	3.164	6.332	9.076
10/26/1992	DJWCAPHI_PORT	2.857	4.891	8.082	13.837
10/29/1993	DJWCAPHI_PORT	3.496	9.065	8.800	22.816
10/31/1994	DJWCAPHI_PORT	5.583	11.849	11.255	23.889
10/30/1995	DJWCAPHI_PORT	11.416	13.297	17.779	20.707
10/28/1996	DJWCAPHI_PORT	10.438	27.768	12.523	33.316
10/27/1997	DJWCAPHI_PORT	33.111	16.369	34.083	16.850
10/26/1998	DJWCAPHI_PORT	19.906	52.803	15.394	40.835
10/29/1999	DJWCAPHI_PORT	29.825	61.826	19.046	39.481
10/30/2000	DJWCAPHI_PORT	−26.119	−27.441	−15.969	−16.777
10/29/2001	DJWCAPHI_PORT	−0.442	−29.014	−0.323	−21.201

9.2% Average Gain

(Continued)

Table 11.3 *(Continued)*

		Five Lowest Net Working Capital			
Date	Port	Apr15 Amnt	AugLTD Amnt	Apr15 Pct	AugLTD Pct
10/27/1975	DJWCAPLOW_PORT	5.587	6.568	35.304	41.500
10/29/1976	DJWCAPLOW_PORT	0.873	−0.112	3.971	−0.510
10/31/1977	DJWCAPLOW_PORT	0.246	2.187	1.166	10.378
10/30/1978	DJWCAPLOW_PORT	1.900	2.745	9.010	13.016
10/29/1979	DJWCAPLOW_PORT	−1.266	3.530	−5.944	16.571
10/27/1980	DJWCAPLOW_PORT	3.914	1.206	15.663	4.826
10/26/1981	DJWCAPLOW_PORT	−0.708	−0.967	−2.857	−3.901
10/29/1982	DJWCAPLOW_PORT	12.617	15.585	46.398	57.314
10/31/1983	DJWCAPLOW_PORT	−1.084	−1.568	−2.141	−3.097
10/29/1984	DJWCAPLOW_PORT	10.010	14.463	21.352	30.852
10/28/1985	DJWCAPLOW_PORT	18.954	8.255	34.708	15.116
10/27/1986	DJWCAPLOW_PORT	17.751	38.335	31.162	67.297
10/26/1987	DJWCAPLOW_PORT	28.313	27.622	48.135	46.961
10/31/1988	DJWCAPLOW_PORT	10.613	14.367	11.800	15.975
10/30/1989	DJWCAPLOW_PORT	5.287	−4.545	5.317	−4.571
10/29/1990	DJWCAPLOW_PORT	19.315	27.073	21.058	29.517
10/28/1991	DJWCAPLOW_PORT	10.984	13.994	8.873	11.305
10/26/1992	DJWCAPLOW_PORT	18.762	20.820	13.753	15.261
10/29/1993	DJWCAPLOW_PORT	−2.469	8.254	−1.478	4.942
10/31/1994	DJWCAPLOW_PORT	26.431	46.010	14.470	25.188
10/30/1995	DJWCAPLOW_PORT	49.118	57.158	19.578	22.783
10/28/1996	DJWCAPLOW_PORT	37.074	78.828	11.769	25.025
10/27/1997	DJWCAPLOW_PORT	108.350	27.737	29.450	7.539
10/26/1998	DJWCAPLOW_PORT	85.308	41.888	19.438	9.544
10/29/1999	DJWCAPLOW_PORT	−29.872	−71.081	−6.219	−14.799
10/30/2000	DJWCAPLOW_PORT	−68.806	−42.182	−15.474	−9.487
10/29/2001	DJWCAPLOW_PORT	26.126	−29.506	6.955	−7.855
					13.9% Average Gain

Table 11.4   Highest and Lowest Price to Net Working Capital in Dow Jones
Industrial Average

| | Five Highest Price to Working Capital | | | |
Date	Port	Apr15 Amnt	AugLTD Amnt	Apr15 Pct	AugLTD Pct
10/27/1975	DJPTOWCAPHI_PORT	10.008	9.977	32.074	31.974
10/29/1976	DJPTOWCAPHI_PORT	2.685	−3.447	6.787	−8.712
10/31/1977	DJPTOWCAPHI_PORT	0.406	7.358	1.230	22.286
10/30/1978	DJPTOWCAPHI_PORT	3.672	7.026	10.346	19.796
10/29/1979	DJPTOWCAPHI_PORT	−5.803	2.581	−15.412	6.856
10/27/1980	DJPTOWCAPHI_PORT	3.165	−6.096	7.790	−15.003
10/26/1981	DJPTOWCAPHI_PORT	−1.191	−4.385	−3.752	−13.819
10/29/1982	DJPTOWCAPHI_PORT	10.414	14.550	36.509	51.008
10/31/1983	DJPTOWCAPHI_PORT	−1.995	−2.862	−3.850	−5.523
10/29/1984	DJPTOWCAPHI_PORT	4.426	12.545	9.749	27.635
10/28/1985	DJPTOWCAPHI_PORT	14.616	5.411	24.095	8.920
10/27/1986	DJPTOWCAPHI_PORT	15.558	35.349	25.950	58.960
10/26/1987	DJPTOWCAPHI_PORT	19.765	23.208	35.584	41.782
10/31/1988	DJPTOWCAPHI_PORT	8.408	15.180	10.090	18.215
10/30/1989	DJPTOWCAPHI_PORT	4.358	1.123	4.692	1.209
10/29/1990	DJPTOWCAPHI_PORT	13.594	21.422	15.098	23.793
10/28/1991	DJPTOWCAPHI_PORT	5.375	7.174	4.865	6.494
10/26/1992	DJPTOWCAPHI_PORT	17.796	15.208	14.849	12.690
10/29/1993	DJPTOWCAPHI_PORT	3.230	28.324	2.268	19.888
10/31/1994	DJPTOWCAPHI_PORT	−2.334	0.617	−1.454	0.384
10/30/1995	DJPTOWCAPHI_PORT	40.783	42.317	25.684	26.650
10/28/1996	DJPTOWCAPHI_PORT	9.235	63.866	4.414	30.527
10/27/1997	DJPTOWCAPHI_PORT	59.173	−14.379	21.639	−5.258
10/26/1998	DJPTOWCAPHI_PORT	34.682	49.325	12.432	17.681
10/29/1999	DJPTOWCAPHI_PORT	−25.415	−45.129	−7.984	−14.177
10/30/2000	DJPTOWCAPHI_PORT	−2.571	−12.425	−0.862	−4.166
10/29/2001	DJPTOWCAPHI_PORT	59.783	17.848	21.947	6.552

10.9% Average Gain

(Continued)

Table 11.4 *(Continued)*

	Five Lowest Net Working Capital				
Date	Port	Apr15 Amnt	AugLTD Amnt	Apr15 Pct	AugLTD Pct
10/27/1975	DJPTOWCAPLOW_PORT	0.415	0.770	17.738	32.895
10/29/1976	DJPTOWCAPLOW_PORT	0.012	0.027	0.397	0.864
10/31/1977	DJPTOWCAPLOW_PORT	0.042	0.354	1.384	11.587
10/30/1978	DJPTOWCAPLOW_PORT	0.235	0.378	7.052	11.342
10/29/1979	DJPTOWCAPLOW_PORT	0.039	0.763	1.131	22.073
10/27/1980	DJPTOWCAPLOW_PORT	0.679	0.376	16.273	9.024
10/26/1981	DJPTOWCAPLOW_PORT	0.110	0.520	2.511	11.829
10/29/1982	DJPTOWCAPLOW_PORT	0.921	1.588	17.262	29.768
10/31/1983	DJPTOWCAPLOW_PORT	0.096	0.941	1.394	13.659
10/29/1984	DJPTOWCAPLOW_PORT	1.345	2.496	17.220	31.962
10/28/1985	DJPTOWCAPLOW_PORT	4.587	5.582	44.053	53.605
10/27/1986	DJPTOWCAPLOW_PORT	4.123	7.098	27.065	46.587
10/26/1987	DJPTOWCAPLOW_PORT	2.811	3.248	18.522	21.401
10/31/1988	DJPTOWCAPLOW_PORT	2.036	5.337	10.237	26.835
10/30/1989	DJPTOWCAPLOW_PORT	1.783	0.507	7.460	2.120
10/29/1990	DJPTOWCAPLOW_PORT	5.322	6.311	22.861	27.110
10/28/1991	DJPTOWCAPLOW_PORT	3.466	4.765	11.685	16.064
10/26/1992	DJPTOWCAPLOW_PORT	1.804	4.352	5.740	13.846
10/29/1993	DJPTOWCAPLOW_PORT	−0.551	1.842	−1.478	4.942
10/31/1994	DJPTOWCAPLOW_PORT	5.900	10.270	14.470	25.188
10/30/1995	DJPTOWCAPLOW_PORT	9.610	12.983	16.989	22.952
10/28/1996	DJPTOWCAPLOW_PORT	8.578	18.240	11.769	25.025
10/27/1997	DJPTOWCAPLOW_PORT	34.848	25.210	40.455	29.266
10/26/1998	DJPTOWCAPLOW_PORT	17.861	4.140	14.584	3.380
10/29/1999	DJPTOWCAPLOW_PORT	−12.673	−25.699	−10.361	−21.012
10/30/2000	DJPTOWCAPLOW_PORT	−9.832	−6.113	−11.065	−6.879
10/29/2001	DJPTOWCAPLOW_PORT	7.613	−3.162	10.029	−4.166
				11.7% Average Gain	

Table 11.5   Measures of Stock Value in Dow Jones Industrial Average

		Five Lowest Cash Flow			
Date	Port	Apr15 Amnt	AugLTD Amnt	Apr15 Pct	AugLTD Pct
10/29/1976	DJCASHFLOW_PORT	0.907	0.363	7.642	3.061
10/31/1977	DJCASHFLOW_PORT	−0.088	0.959	−0.756	8.239
10/30/1978	DJCASHFLOW_PORT	1.432	2.219	11.956	18.523
10/29/1979	DJCASHFLOW_PORT	−1.084	1.850	−8.620	14.708
10/27/1980	DJCASHFLOW_PORT	−1.340	−2.326	−9.533	−16.552
10/26/1981	DJCASHFLOW_PORT	−2.379	−2.348	−22.616	−22.324
10/29/1982	DJCASHFLOW_PORT	3.198	4.816	37.762	56.877
10/31/1983	DJCASHFLOW_PORT	0.406	−0.171	2.674	−1.124
10/29/1984	DJCASHFLOW_PORT	1.414	1.939	9.948	13.643
10/28/1985	DJCASHFLOW_PORT	5.019	0.245	33.634	1.641
10/27/1986	DJCASHFLOW_PORT	3.232	5.817	22.553	40.590
10/26/1987	DJCASHFLOW_PORT	5.843	6.313	45.741	49.422
10/31/1988	DJCASHFLOW_PORT	2.214	6.082	10.800	29.667
10/30/1989	DJCASHFLOW_PORT	1.721	−0.645	7.140	−2.675
10/29/1990	DJCASHFLOW_PORT	5.785	7.261	27.717	34.786
10/28/1991	DJCASHFLOW_PORT	−1.377	−2.080	−4.925	−7.438
10/26/1992	DJCASHFLOW_PORT	2.797	2.938	11.067	11.624
10/29/1993	DJCASHFLOW_PORT	−0.176	1.507	−0.587	5.030
10/31/1994	DJCASHFLOW_PORT	2.007	4.336	6.947	15.007
10/30/1995	DJCASHFLOW_PORT	7.162	5.655	21.719	17.149
10/28/1996	DJCASHFLOW_PORT	2.521	6.997	6.476	17.976
10/27/1997	DJCASHFLOW_PORT	18.279	2.767	41.939	6.348
10/26/1998	DJCASHFLOW_PORT	12.698	15.437	25.001	30.393
10/29/1999	DJCASHFLOW_PORT	−5.562	6.268	−8.116	9.147
10/30/2000	DJCASHFLOW_PORT	−6.802	−7.703	−9.522	−10.784
10/29/2001	DJCASHFLOW_PORT	8.933	−6.194	15.513	−10.757

10.8% Average Gain

(Continued)

Table 11.5 *(Continued)*

	Five Lowest Price to Sales				
Date	Port	Apr15 Amnt	AugLTD Amnt	Apr15 Pct	AugLTD Pct
10/27/1975	DJPTOSALES_PORT	0.338	0.670	12.703	25.177
10/29/1976	DJPTOSALES_PORT	0.294	0.329	8.818	9.891
10/31/1977	DJPTOSALES_PORT	0.021	0.349	0.615	9.981
10/30/1978	DJPTOSALES_PORT	0.357	0.877	9.662	23.748
10/29/1979	DJPTOSALES_PORT	0.123	0.961	2.826	22.152
10/27/1980	DJPTOSALES_PORT	0.319	0.066	6.059	1.252
10/26/1981	DJPTOSALES_PORT	0.500	1.178	10.003	23.542
10/29/1982	DJPTOSALES_PORT	1.469	2.316	21.295	33.569
10/31/1983	DJPTOSALES_PORT	0.740	1.039	8.162	11.467
10/29/1984	DJPTOSALES_PORT	1.587	2.110	16.245	21.591
10/28/1985	DJPTOSALES_PORT	3.977	6.250	33.269	52.290
10/27/1986	DJPTOSALES_PORT	3.602	8.283	20.348	46.791
10/26/1987	DJPTOSALES_PORT	1.878	2.540	9.953	13.458
10/31/1988	DJPTOSALES_PORT	2.267	8.623	9.773	37.183
10/30/1989	DJPTOSALES_PORT	1.618	0.339	5.115	1.071
10/29/1990	DJPTOSALES_PORT	12.121	12.911	41.938	44.670
10/28/1991	DJPTOSALES_PORT	3.127	1.905	7.972	4.857
10/26/1992	DJPTOSALES_PORT	5.989	9.313	15.204	23.641
10/29/1993	DJPTOSALES_PORT	3.368	7.546	6.894	15.445
10/31/1994	DJPTOSALES_PORT	7.456	14.259	13.264	25.366
10/30/1995	DJPTOSALES_PORT	13.788	13.243	18.871	18.124
10/28/1996	DJPTOSALES_PORT	7.913	33.482	8.377	35.445
10/27/1997	DJPTOSALES_PORT	49.981	36.878	39.163	28.896
10/26/1998	DJPTOSALES_PORT	58.751	74.503	31.813	40.343
10/29/1999	DJPTOSALES_PORT	10.288	29.095	3.967	11.219
10/30/2000	DJPTOSALES_PORT	−13.687	−11.244	−4.680	−3.845
10/29/2001	DJPTOSALES_PORT	18.606	−16.780	7.101	−6.404

13.5% Average Gain

Table 11.5   *(Continued)*

		Five Highest Dividend Yield			
Date	Port	Apr15 Amnt	AugLTD Amnt	Apr15 Pct	AugLTD Pct
10/27/1975	DJDIVYIELD_PORT	1.978	2.987	21.119	31.886
10/29/1976	DJDIVYIELD_PORT	0.767	0.543	6.136	4.349
10/31/1977	DJDIVYIELD_PORT	0.418	1.352	3.384	10.935
10/30/1978	DJDIVYIELD_PORT	3.193	4.437	24.955	34.670
10/29/1979	DJDIVYIELD_PORT	−1.004	2.836	−6.277	17.729
10/27/1980	DJDIVYIELD_PORT	2.471	1.802	13.204	9.626
10/26/1981	DJDIVYIELD_PORT	−0.113	−1.654	−0.572	−8.366
10/29/1982	DJDIVYIELD_PORT	4.096	6.524	19.953	31.778
10/31/1983	DJDIVYIELD_PORT	3.265	3.830	12.163	14.265
10/29/1984	DJDIVYIELD_PORT	1.580	5.462	5.249	18.147
10/28/1985	DJDIVYIELD_PORT	6.267	10.443	16.920	28.197
10/27/1986	DJDIVYIELD_PORT	11.704	18.944	25.218	40.817
10/26/1987	DJDIVYIELD_PORT	12.741	13.589	28.103	29.973
10/31/1988	DJDIVYIELD_PORT	5.370	16.630	8.585	26.587
10/30/1989	DJDIVYIELD_PORT	5.293	1.853	6.925	2.424
10/29/1990	DJDIVYIELD_PORT	19.536	41.425	27.684	58.703
10/28/1991	DJDIVYIELD_PORT	17.260	20.682	15.677	18.785
10/26/1992	DJDIVYIELD_PORT	17.317	28.570	14.262	23.530
10/29/1993	DJDIVYIELD_PORT	−2.881	20.012	−1.865	12.955
10/31/1994	DJDIVYIELD_PORT	12.418	40.952	7.047	23.240
10/30/1995	DJDIVYIELD_PORT	45.707	62.689	20.101	27.569
10/28/1996	DJDIVYIELD_PORT	33.354	92.049	10.596	29.242
10/27/1997	DJDIVYIELD_PORT	79.415	46.908	20.346	12.018
10/26/1998	DJDIVYIELD_PORT	80.749	92.945	16.613	19.122
10/29/1999	DJDIVYIELD_PORT	−38.375	22.936	−6.805	4.067
10/30/2000	DJDIVYIELD_PORT	37.913	57.500	6.659	10.099
10/29/2001	DJDIVYIELD_PORT	90.205	5.719	16.897	1.071
				12.3% Average Gain	

Table 11.6 Return on Dow Jones Industrial Average Stocks

| | | Return on Five Highest Cash Flow | | | |
Date	Port	Apr15 Amnt	AugLTD Amnt	Apr15 Pct	AugLTD Pct
10/29/1976	DJCASHFLOW_PORT	−0.003	−2.062	−0.029	−17.722
10/31/1977	DJCASHFLOW_PORT	−0.013	0.618	−0.141	6.911
10/30/1978	DJCASHFLOW_PORT	1.822	2.155	21.037	24.880
10/29/1979	DJCASHFLOW_PORT	0.330	2.446	3.260	24.141
10/27/1980	DJCASHFLOW_PORT	2.449	1.160	19.504	9.233
10/26/1981	DJCASHFLOW_PORT	0.993	0.698	7.905	5.553
10/29/1982	DJCASHFLOW_PORT	3.103	6.769	21.140	46.116
10/31/1983	DJCASHFLOW_PORT	−1.483	−1.206	−7.279	−5.921
10/29/1984	DJCASHFLOW_PORT	−0.282	1.781	−1.617	10.230
10/28/1985	DJCASHFLOW_PORT	2.007	4.789	10.516	25.099
10/27/1986	DJCASHFLOW_PORT	6.886	16.800	29.595	72.203
10/26/1987	DJCASHFLOW_PORT	8.353	7.079	33.272	28.197
10/31/1988	DJCASHFLOW_PORT	2.400	9.848	7.306	29.976
10/30/1989	DJCASHFLOW_PORT	0.212	−7.709	0.501	−18.251
10/29/1990	DJCASHFLOW_PORT	8.284	9.638	26.975	31.384
10/28/1991	DJCASHFLOW_PORT	11.178	7.335	28.391	18.629
10/26/1992	DJCASHFLOW_PORT	4.623	8.195	10.064	17.841
10/29/1993	DJCASHFLOW_PORT	4.924	13.820	8.936	25.079
10/31/1994	DJCASHFLOW_PORT	2.612	4.851	3.668	6.811
10/30/1995	DJCASHFLOW_PORT	15.366	21.022	19.573	26.776
10/28/1996	DJCASHFLOW_PORT	4.133	23.400	3.811	21.578
10/27/1997	DJCASHFLOW_PORT	19.788	−18.546	15.480	−14.509
10/26/1998	DJCASHFLOW_PORT	17.406	11.193	14.035	9.025
10/29/1999	DJCASHFLOW_PORT	−2.337	−5.375	−1.734	−3.988
10/30/2000	DJCASHFLOW_PORT	0.716	5.940	0.538	4.465
10/29/2001	DJCASHFLOW_PORT	20.598	−7.248	16.145	−5.681

11.2% Average Gain

Table 11.6   *(Continued)*

		Return on Five Highest Consecutive Earnings Growth			
Date	Port	Apr15 Amnt	AugLTD Amnt	Apr15 Pct	AugLTD Pct
10/29/1976	DJEARNGROW_PORT	0.152	0.251	4.765	7.872
10/31/1977	DJEARNGROW_PORT	0.005	0.731	0.151	22.532
10/30/1978	DJEARNGROW_PORT	0.082	0.348	2.263	9.654
10/29/1979	DJEARNGROW_PORT	−0.087	0.664	−2.415	18.502
10/27/1980	DJEARNGROW_PORT	0.749	0.279	18.420	6.858
10/26/1981	DJEARNGROW_PORT	0.374	1.068	8.503	24.252
10/29/1982	DJEARNGROW_PORT	1.069	1.081	17.355	17.549
10/31/1983	DJEARNGROW_PORT	−0.149	0.696	−1.984	9.278
10/29/1984	DJEARNGROW_PORT	0.605	1.782	7.298	21.507
10/28/1985	DJEARNGROW_PORT	3.890	5.623	34.423	49.756
10/27/1986	DJEARNGROW_PORT	4.673	10.073	29.343	63.251
10/26/1987	DJEARNGROW_PORT	1.009	1.395	5.587	7.720
10/31/1988	DJEARNGROW_PORT	3.540	8.625	16.813	40.966
10/30/1989	DJEARNGROW_PORT	2.563	1.568	8.617	5.272
10/29/1990	DJEARNGROW_PORT	10.919	12.800	37.390	43.834
10/28/1991	DJEARNGROW_PORT	6.679	6.916	15.923	16.488
10/26/1992	DJEARNGROW_PORT	−0.664	2.276	−1.439	4.931
10/29/1993	DJEARNGROW_PORT	−0.806	3.675	−1.576	7.186
10/31/1994	DJEARNGROW_PORT	9.552	17.447	17.146	31.316
10/30/1995	DJEARNGROW_PORT	13.764	17.102	16.900	20.999
10/28/1996	DJEARNGROW_PORT	17.902	29.799	16.764	27.906
10/27/1997	DJEARNGROW_PORT	44.369	29.537	35.274	23.482
10/26/1998	DJEARNGROW_PORT	70.982	54.210	39.957	30.516
10/29/1999	DJEARNGROW_PORT	−19.798	−9.354	−7.700	−3.638
10/30/2000	DJEARNGROW_PORT	−22.091	−21.000	−8.616	−8.191
10/29/2001	DJEARNGROW_PORT	19.876	−33.235	8.975	−15.007

12.2% Average Gain

(Continued)

Table 11.6 *(Continued)*

		Return on Five Highest Projected One-Year Earnings			
Date	Port	Apr15 Amnt	AugLTD Amnt	Apr15 Pct	AugLTD Pct
10/29/1976	DJFUTEARN_PORT	3.348	−5.307	6.889	−10.919
10/31/1977	DJFUTEARN_PORT	0.677	6.349	1.649	15.458
10/30/1978	DJFUTEARN_PORT	2.822	6.060	6.763	14.523
10/29/1979	DJFUTEARN_PORT	−5.524	4.250	−12.893	9.920
10/27/1980	DJFUTEARN_PORT	−1.316	−5.967	−2.810	−12.739
10/26/1981	DJFUTEARN_PORT	−1.860	−2.619	−4.930	−6.942
10/29/1982	DJFUTEARN_PORT	3.111	4.837	8.601	13.374
10/31/1983	DJFUTEARN_PORT	−2.538	1.243	−5.949	2.914
10/29/1984	DJFUTEARN_PORT	6.269	10.126	14.619	23.615
10/28/1985	DJFUTEARN_PORT	14.001	5.890	25.105	10.561
10/27/1986	DJFUTEARN_PORT	11.191	23.416	19.244	40.267
10/26/1987	DJFUTEARN_PORT	13.592	11.885	26.827	23.458
10/31/1988	DJFUTEARN_PORT	7.655	7.943	11.619	12.055
10/30/1989	DJFUTEARN_PORT	0.243	−8.899	0.402	−14.752
10/29/1990	DJFUTEARN_PORT	5.920	9.032	13.200	20.141
10/28/1991	DJFUTEARN_PORT	1.443	4.262	2.866	8.467
10/26/1992	DJFUTEARN_PORT	8.815	15.529	15.718	27.691
10/29/1993	DJFUTEARN_PORT	−3.302	−2.817	−4.587	−3.912
10/31/1994	DJFUTEARN_PORT	2.431	5.558	3.664	8.379
10/30/1995	DJFUTEARN_PORT	16.325	11.752	23.603	16.992
10/28/1996	DJFUTEARN_PORT	6.919	15.426	8.226	18.338
10/27/1997	DJFUTEARN_PORT	10.027	−12.982	10.411	−13.480
10/26/1998	DJFUTEARN_PORT	22.358	20.248	24.558	22.241
10/29/1999	DJFUTEARN_PORT	1.799	13.824	1.697	13.036
10/30/2000	DJFUTEARN_PORT	2.009	4.667	1.983	4.607
10/29/2001	DJFUTEARN_PORT	12.193	5.985	12.532	6.152

8.0% Average Gain

Table 11.6   *(Continued)*

		Return on Five Lowest Price to Book			
Date	Port	Apr15 Amnt	AugLTD Amnt	Apr15 Pct	AugLTD Pct
10/27/1975	DJPRICEBOOK_PORT	2.162	3.163	26.262	38.413
10/29/1976	DJPRICEBOOK_PORT	1.625	−0.797	15.338	−7.523
10/31/1977	DJPRICEBOOK_PORT	0.183	1.875	2.020	20.716
10/30/1978	DJPRICEBOOK_PORT	2.387	2.267	25.467	24.186
10/29/1979	DJPRICEBOOK_PORT	−1.313	1.595	−12.662	15.379
10/27/1980	DJPRICEBOOK_PORT	2.322	−0.260	18.855	−2.115
10/26/1981	DJPRICEBOOK_PORT	−1.129	−2.840	−10.293	−25.897
10/29/1982	DJPRICEBOOK_PORT	4.075	5.667	46.123	64.149
10/31/1983	DJPRICEBOOK_PORT	0.384	−0.445	2.346	−2.720
10/29/1984	DJPRICEBOOK_PORT	2.154	2.136	15.120	14.990
10/28/1985	DJPRICEBOOK_PORT	3.801	0.963	25.172	6.377
10/27/1986	DJPRICEBOOK_PORT	3.817	9.914	25.330	65.796
10/26/1987	DJPRICEBOOK_PORT	8.789	9.081	61.009	63.035
10/31/1988	DJPRICEBOOK_PORT	2.655	6.924	10.731	27.985
10/30/1989	DJPRICEBOOK_PORT	2.167	−3.008	7.186	−9.974
10/29/1990	DJPRICEBOOK_PORT	10.399	20.143	41.607	80.594
10/28/1991	DJPRICEBOOK_PORT	9.904	3.973	21.673	8.693
10/26/1992	DJPRICEBOOK_PORT	8.248	14.636	15.864	28.150
10/29/1993	DJPRICEBOOK_PORT	2.967	11.515	4.332	16.818
10/31/1994	DJPRICEBOOK_PORT	8.112	22.306	9.998	27.490
10/30/1995	DJPRICEBOOK_PORT	29.396	32.808	27.865	31.099
10/28/1996	DJPRICEBOOK_PORT	4.640	51.322	3.050	33.728
10/27/1997	DJPRICEBOOK_PORT	35.277	−26.503	18.378	−13.807
10/26/1998	DJPRICEBOOK_PORT	47.435	49.443	25.173	26.239
10/29/1999	DJPRICEBOOK_PORT	6.703	28.613	2.805	11.972
10/30/2000	DJPRICEBOOK_PORT	16.471	37.933	6.122	14.100
10/29/2001	DJPRICEBOOK_PORT	38.373	−21.448	14.028	−7.841

16.6% Average Gain

(Continued)

Table 11.6 *(Continued)*

		Return on Five Highest Return on Equity			
Date	Port	Apr15 Amnt	AugLTD Amnt	Apr15 Pct	AugLTD Pct
10/27/1975	DJRTNEQTY_PORT	2.755	3.468	30.152	37.958
10/29/1976	DJRTNEQTY_PORT	−0.481	−0.428	−3.980	−3.543
10/31/1977	DJRTNEQTY_PORT	0.189	2.235	1.725	20.387
10/30/1978	DJRTNEQTY_PORT	0.144	0.988	1.194	8.212
10/29/1979	DJRTNEQTY_PORT	−0.494	1.870	−4.219	15.978
10/27/1980	DJRTNEQTY_PORT	1.914	0.218	14.570	1.661
10/26/1981	DJRTNEQTY_PORT	0.321	1.167	2.549	9.266
10/29/1982	DJRTNEQTY_PORT	4.869	6.985	32.340	46.391
10/31/1983	DJRTNEQTY_PORT	−3.426	0.201	−12.855	0.755
10/29/1984	DJRTNEQTY_PORT	2.079	2.052	7.715	7.616
10/28/1985	DJRTNEQTY_PORT	15.071	16.821	52.858	58.994
10/27/1986	DJRTNEQTY_PORT	10.862	23.057	25.992	55.177
10/26/1987	DJRTNEQTY_PORT	5.035	8.472	11.335	19.073
10/31/1988	DJRTNEQTY_PORT	8.692	18.793	15.615	33.759
10/30/1989	DJRTNEQTY_PORT	0.939	1.444	1.300	2.000
10/29/1990	DJRTNEQTY_PORT	17.978	27.163	24.644	37.235
10/28/1991	DJRTNEQTY_PORT	17.785	18.340	17.598	18.147
10/26/1992	DJRTNEQTY_PORT	−14.552	−10.718	−12.369	−9.110
10/29/1993	DJRTNEQTY_PORT	−7.542	8.000	−6.804	7.216
10/31/1994	DJRTNEQTY_PORT	10.746	25.442	8.757	20.734
10/30/1995	DJRTNEQTY_PORT	27.481	33.961	17.856	22.067
10/28/1996	DJRTNEQTY_PORT	28.137	55.539	14.294	28.215
10/27/1997	DJRTNEQTY_PORT	66.222	28.513	31.001	13.348
10/26/1998	DJRTNEQTY_PORT	15.585	13.512	5.739	4.975
10/29/1999	DJRTNEQTY_PORT	−30.689	18.197	−10.714	6.353
10/30/2000	DJRTNEQTY_PORT	11.476	6.485	3.702	2.092
10/29/2001	DJRTNEQTY_PORT	1.611	−43.309	0.534	−14.364

10.0% Average Gain

Table 11.6 *(Continued)*

		Return on Five Highest Sales per Employee			
Date	Port	Apr15 Amnt	AugLTD Amnt	Apr15 Pct	AugLTD Pct
10/27/1975	DJSALESEMP_PORT	0.814	1.230	14.018	21.167
10/29/1976	DJSALESEMP_PORT	0.002	0.226	0.031	3.257
10/31/1977	DJSALESEMP_PORT	−0.069	0.545	−0.985	7.760
10/30/1978	DJSALESEMP_PORT	0.758	1.605	10.446	22.114
10/29/1979	DJSALESEMP_PORT	0.643	2.273	7.570	26.765
10/27/1980	DJSALESEMP_PORT	−0.004	0.100	−0.038	0.887
10/26/1981	DJSALESEMP_PORT	0.400	0.976	3.559	8.692
10/29/1982	DJSALESEMP_PORT	2.511	3.421	18.641	25.390
10/31/1983	DJSALESEMP_PORT	0.824	1.632	5.004	9.911
10/29/1984	DJSALESEMP_PORT	2.101	3.682	12.023	21.066
10/28/1985	DJSALESEMP_PORT	1.999	5.588	8.961	25.054
10/27/1986	DJSALESEMP_PORT	5.799	10.898	21.685	40.755
10/26/1987	DJSALESEMP_PORT	7.665	7.426	30.063	29.122
10/31/1988	DJSALESEMP_PORT	4.597	8.339	13.698	24.849
10/30/1989	DJSALESEMP_PORT	3.635	4.993	8.367	11.494
10/29/1990	DJSALESEMP_PORT	13.746	12.519	30.315	27.609
10/28/1991	DJSALESEMP_PORT	6.494	10.446	11.289	18.159
10/26/1992	DJSALESEMP_PORT	7.013	10.516	10.392	15.583
10/29/1993	DJSALESEMP_PORT	0.905	11.161	1.132	13.958
10/31/1994	DJSALESEMP_PORT	4.722	13.195	5.003	13.979
10/30/1995	DJSALESEMP_PORT	24.749	31.021	21.619	27.097
10/28/1996	DJSALESEMP_PORT	17.156	37.555	11.067	24.226
10/27/1997	DJSALESEMP_PORT	36.017	3.979	19.427	2.146
10/26/1998	DJSALESEMP_PORT	40.768	43.103	20.260	21.421
10/29/1999	DJSALESEMP_PORT	15.255	57.924	6.150	23.352
10/30/2000	DJSALESEMP_PORT	−42.553	−53.828	−14.491	−18.331
10/29/2001	DJSALESEMP_PORT	15.912	−18.379	6.796	−7.850

10.4% Average Gain

(Continued)

Table 11.6 *(Continued)*

		Return on Five Lowest Price to One-Year Forward Earnings			
Date	Port	Apr15 Amnt	AugLTD Amnt	Apr15 Pct	AugLTD Pct
10/29/1976	DJPTOEARN_PORT	1.567	−1.810	10.583	−12.222
10/31/1977	DJPTOEARN_PORT	0.856	3.714	6.950	30.153
10/30/1978	DJPTOEARN_PORT	2.969	4.266	22.152	31.830
10/29/1979	DJPTOEARN_PORT	−0.909	2.735	−5.840	17.576
10/27/1980	DJPTOEARN_PORT	0.964	−2.044	5.073	−10.761
10/26/1981	DJPTOEARN_PORT	0.872	1.668	5.554	10.629
10/29/1982	DJPTOEARN_PORT	6.824	9.409	36.116	49.794
10/31/1983	DJPTOEARN_PORT	−1.918	0.578	−5.722	1.723
10/29/1984	DJPTOEARN_PORT	3.723	4.423	11.243	13.356
10/28/1985	DJPTOEARN_PORT	11.193	10.539	33.583	31.621
10/27/1986	DJPTOEARN_PORT	13.499	31.404	29.617	68.903
10/26/1987	DJPTOEARN_PORT	23.278	21.375	53.603	49.221
10/31/1988	DJPTOEARN_PORT	6.472	7.998	9.666	11.944
10/30/1989	DJPTOEARN_PORT	−1.263	−12.097	−2.107	−20.185
10/29/1990	DJPTOEARN_PORT	19.016	26.896	45.333	64.118
10/28/1991	DJPTOEARN_PORT	13.165	6.443	21.606	10.575
10/26/1992	DJPTOEARN_PORT	13.468	20.111	20.322	30.348
10/29/1993	DJPTOEARN_PORT	−0.794	5.787	−0.923	6.730
10/31/1994	DJPTOEARN_PORT	3.623	18.351	4.010	20.310
10/30/1995	DJPTOEARN_PORT	18.662	7.884	17.773	7.508
10/28/1996	DJPTOEARN_PORT	9.942	31.381	8.675	27.382
10/27/1997	DJPTOEARN_PORT	32.709	0.006	21.906	0.004
10/26/1998	DJPTOEARN_PORT	42.216	31.200	25.406	18.776
10/29/1999	DJPTOEARN_PORT	−12.283	7.341	−6.805	4.067
10/30/2000	DJPTOEARN_PORT	18.946	33.589	10.265	18.198
10/29/2001	DJPTOEARN_PORT	37.885	0.224	19.870	0.117

15.3% Average Gain

Table 11.6   *(Continued)*

| | | Return on Five Highest Price to Sales | | | |
Date	Port	Apr15 Amnt	AugLTD Amnt	Apr15 Pct	AugLTD Pct
10/27/1975	DJPTOSALES_PORT	9.613	9.735	25.710	26.037
10/29/1976	DJPTOSALES_PORT	0.668	−6.394	1.409	−13.481
10/31/1977	DJPTOSALES_PORT	−0.287	6.981	−0.775	18.827
10/30/1978	DJPTOSALES_PORT	4.335	8.402	11.126	21.563
10/29/1979	DJPTOSALES_PORT	−2.904	5.806	−6.973	13.942
10/27/1980	DJPTOSALES_PORT	0.792	−7.432	1.713	−16.088
10/26/1981	DJPTOSALES_PORT	−1.971	−5.250	−5.828	−15.522
10/29/1982	DJPTOSALES_PORT	10.173	14.230	33.343	46.640
10/31/1983	DJPTOSALES_PORT	−3.367	−2.329	−6.607	−4.571
10/29/1984	DJPTOSALES_PORT	7.782	15.818	17.447	35.464
10/28/1985	DJPTOSALES_PORT	20.212	4.226	32.865	6.871
10/27/1986	DJPTOSALES_PORT	16.988	29.561	28.329	49.295
10/26/1987	DJPTOSALES_PORT	12.234	8.970	21.764	15.957
10/31/1988	DJPTOSALES_PORT	8.531	10.939	12.556	16.101
10/30/1989	DJPTOSALES_PORT	6.686	−5.620	10.235	−8.604
10/29/1990	DJPTOSALES_PORT	13.197	12.457	23.479	22.164
10/28/1991	DJPTOSALES_PORT	2.35	−0.252	3.436	−0.369
10/26/1992	DJPTOSALES_PORT	12.229	8.133	17.568	11.684
10/29/1993	DJPTOSALES_PORT	4.415	17.956	5.426	22.067
10/31/1994	DJPTOSALES_PORT	0.866	5.298	0.922	5.642
10/30/1995	DJPTOSALES_PORT	19.705	13.079	19.590	13.002
10/28/1996	DJPTOSALES_PORT	9.230	26.701	8.186	23.682
10/27/1997	DJPTOSALES_PORT	18.407	−9.881	13.541	−7.268
10/26/1998	DJPTOSALES_PORT	20.516	32.075	15.609	24.404
10/29/1999	DJPTOSALES_PORT	−13.465	−10.677	−8.493	−6.734
10/30/2000	DJPTOSALES_PORT	−5.533	−4.319	−3.774	−2.946
10/29/2001	DJPTOSALES_PORT	16.109	3.301	12.115	2.483
					10.5% Average Gain

wide array of values so you can see the difference and impact these ratios have upon typical market performance. As an example, this strategy on the five highest cash flow stocks averaged 11.2 percent while on the lowest it averaged 10.8 percent. Looks like a push to me.

The five lowest price-to-sales stocks returned 13.5 percent while the highest price-to-sales mustered up only 10.5 percent. That's quite a difference.

Many analysts say it all boils down to consecutive earnings growth. Could be, but my studies show an average gain of 12.2 percent; good, but there are better value measures. One that surprised me was the measure of return on equity. I thought a high rate of return on a company's equity would be a great sign of future price appreciation. That is not the case from this study, which reflects a rather modest 10.0 percent return; one would do better to look at the ratio of sales per employee, which returned 10.4 percent.

Anyway, here they all are for your perusal, study, and edification. At times I update these studies on my web site at www.larrywms.com.

The beauty of these ratios is that they keep us out of trouble. We do not walk down the disturbing dark alleys of Wall Street. Intelligent investors don't want risk; they want return. And we now have a way of eliminating a good deal of the risk. Do that and it means it is mathematically impossible for our returns not to be greater than those of someone just buying the averages.

In other words, you can do what the average guy and what 80 percent of the mutual funds have not been able to do—you can beat the market! This is a staggering statement when you consider that 80 percent of the funds cannot outperform the S&P 500 or the Dow Jones Industrial Average. Funds don't appear to be such a great investment. Knowing that only 20 percent of fund managers can beat the market tells us that we have only a 20 percent chance of selecting the right fund. Eight times out of 10 the fund we select will not do as well as just buying the Dow Jones Industrial Average. This is staggering.

The various ratios shown here can be used to evaluate any stock, at any time. Maybe it's a hot tip from your broker or brother-in-law. It may be good. The proof comes from checking the valuation numbers shown here. You can prove this to yourself by listening to CNBC or the Neil Cavuto show on Fox. The next time you hear of a stock that is falling out of bed, check the valuations. Invariably, when I do this fun exercise, what I see are stocks with horrible valuations—a reason for the crash.

The opposite of this is that by using some very simple rules we can consistently outperform the Dow and in the process outperform the fund managers. We can do this without paying the fund managers their excessive fees, without being exposed to a basket of stocks we know nothing about and to any possible chicanery on the part of wrongly intentioned fund managers. If the odds are 8 to 2 against us beating the market through the mutual funds process, why not do it on our own?

There is only one reason: You haven't known how to. But that is now a thing of the past. You can beat the market averages. You can outperform the hotshots of Wall Street.

MORE ON MUTUAL FUNDS

It's no secret the mutual funds that made so much money during the last bull market lost a ton during the bear market. This tells us that past performance is sure as heck no guarantee of future success. Here's more proof. In a study I did of the best-performing funds for the past three years—2002, 2001, and 2000—the four best-performing funds for 2002 had actually underperformed the S&P 500 in 1998 and 1999, the big bull years! Had you gone by their performance in the good years, you would never have bought them for the bad years. Ah, yes, the first one now shall later be last.

THE WILLIAMS WAY TO BEAT WALL STREET

The ratio figures set up for us the ideal investment scenario. As we can see, the best group of stocks to buy, on average, would be those with the lowest price and highest yield in the average or sector we're purchasing. So that's our first criterion. We have answered the selection aspect of investing by knowing exactly what stocks perform, overall, better than the averages. The rule is simple: Buy the low-priced one with the highest current yield or lowest price-to-sales ratio.

I took this one step further by adding a timing mechanism of when to buy and sell our select list, the hot stocks if you will, from the investment average. Earlier in this book I showed there is a distinct tendency for the Dow Jones Industrial Average to rally from October into the spring of the year.

Now let me show you the real kicker here, which is what the Dow Jones Utility Average does.

As you can see in Figure 11.2, the vast majority of the time the utility index starts a big rally just about the time the stock market stops going up or goes into a sideways trading zone. Generally speaking, this usually begins in about April of each year. From April into the October low the stock market typically doesn't perform nearly as well. Yes, some years it doesn't follow this tendency and continues churning higher. But that is the exception. Smart investors don't bet on the exception.

The utility index usually starts a big up move around the first week of April into the first week of October.

Thus, we have a rolling investment program going on here. The data presented next reflects that of buying the Dow Jones Industrial Average the last week of October of each year, exiting on the first Friday of April the next year, and at that time purchasing the five lowest-priced and highest-yield Dow Jones Utility stocks of each year, holding until the first trading week of Octo-

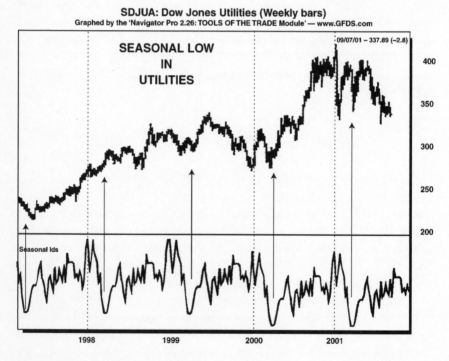

Figure 11.2 Dow Jones Utilities

ber. That portfolio has achieved remarkable gains far surpassing anything the mutual funds have done, and has been doing so on a consistent basis.

LARRY WILLIAMS HIGH-YIELD INVESTMENT

This approach, timing the entry and exiting into the high-yield, low-priced stocks switching from one Dow Jones average, to another has averaged 24.1 percent a year since 1985 (see Table 11.7). I do have figures that go back further than this that suggest an equally high rate of return. The Dow Jones Industrial Average from 1976 to 2001 had a net showing of

Table 11.7   Rolling Investment Program

Year	% Return Buying Utilities at Seasonal Low, Exiting at Seasonal High	% Return Buying Industrials at Seasonal Low, Exiting at Seasonal High	% Return Buy and Hold Dow 30	% Return Dow Jones Industrial Average
1985	5.90	24.495	30.8	28
1986	5.330	29.998	35.2	25
1987	−0.202	−7.824	−8.0	0
1988	11.2	13.161	24.3	11
1989	19.809	9.182	28.9	29.4
1990	−1.843	20.919	19.0	−5
1991	3.957	14.399	18.2	18
1992	0.774	25.037	25.8	3
1993	6.444	2.413	8.8	14
1994	−6.142	12.963	6.7	2
1995	8.537	14.896	23.3	33
1996	4.750	17.879	21.8	28
1997	19.486	18.905	38.3	17
1998	13.42	19.377	32.7	19
1999	3.692	7.709	11.3	24
2000	35.8	5.4	54.8	−6
2001	13.9–7/2001	17.7	30.9	−5
		Average	24.1	13.8

8.3 percent a year. During that same time our continual rolling program would have done close to 30 percent a year.

The beauty of the program, I believe, comes from a combination of two factors. We are sidestepping the time period when stocks, at least in the Dow Jones Industrial Average, are most susceptible to decline. We are not invested in that danger zone. Instead of being invested in the industrials at that time we're investing in the utility stocks, which typically pay a higher rate of return than the Dow Jones Industrial Average stocks and also have less volatility to the downside during market declines. There is a fundamental reason for this: Utility stocks offer investors a yield, a rate of return, as opposed to long-term capital appreciation.

This is why the utilities actually outperform the Dow Jones Industrial Average most of the time during this danger zone. The reason is simple. When stocks start to slide, people get out of the Dow Jones Industrial Average looking for a safer haven for their money. That is exactly what the utilities offer, a higher rate of return and some possible upside appreciation, so money flows from the Dow Jones Industrial Average into the utility stocks. Our investment program simply has us getting aboard utility stocks just a little bit before the stock market usually declines.

It's not often in this life that we are able to get the best of both worlds. But the Williams way to beat Wall Street by design can do exactly that by combining what we know about the market on a long-term cyclical basis with what we know about it on a fundamental basis.

From this we also learn that at major stock market lows we want to invest in the lowest-priced, highest-yield stocks. Not all market lows come in October. You'll see plenty of other buying opportunities as the markets unfold over the next 20 to 100 years. But at the low junctures, instead of trying to buy yesteryear's leaders, why not buy stable, solid blue-chip type stocks? These are the safer ones; these are the ones that are more predictable, more precise, and have a lot better chance of staying in business, of weathering the storms.

Utility stocks don't lead or begin this new bull market; they simply are more resistant to declines than are industrial or blue-chip stocks. The beginning of a bull market first lifts up blue-chip and growth stocks. These stocks will substantially outperform other issues in the popular market averages. So we know the general category of stocks to invest in.

That part of our selection process is pretty simple. The next step is to go to your local library and get *Investor's Business Daily* or *Value Line* to determine from any list of blue-chip and growth stocks the ones that currently have the lowest prices and highest dividend yields. These are the safest, most secure stocks to purchase. Again, others may outperform you on a short-term basis, on the first leg of a bull market, that type of thing, but over the long term you will beat the pants off of them. You will do this because they are not consistent and they will end up buying some turkey stocks along the way—stocks that not only don't go up but also have substantial down moves despite the overall bull market. If you wanted to make absolutely certain you are buying the best stocks at the junctures, you would also check that infamous price-to-sales ratio to make certain that you are buying stocks that have a price-to-sales ratios below 1.0, as we know that the danger of buying high price-to-sales ratio stocks is extreme.

LAZY PERSON'S GUIDE TO BEATING THE FUNDS

Should you decide not to try to pick individual stocks, there is still an easy way to beat the market by beating the funds.

The concept is simple; since the funds are not that great themselves, and are always subject to sizable down moves, all we need to do is develop a timing system or technique that allows us to buy and sell mutual funds so we are with them for the up moves and in cash, on the sidelines, when the funds decline.

This is a most interesting concept—we leave stock picking to supposed experts! Our effort will be to select funds that advance rapidly in market up moves, then liquidate our positions before a substantial decline.

We have three challenges in this case. First, instead of finding a hot stock, we will want to find mutual funds that have historically done very well in market up moves. Second, these funds will charge us no, or a very low, commission or fee for moving from a long position to cash. Third, we will need some sort of system or tool to tell us it's time to lock up our profits when trouble in the way of a down move may be just around the corner.

There are several rating services of mutual fund performance, but the sad truth is that their ratings have very little to do with a given fund's future performance.

Take the hugely successful Morningstar service. If you have ever read advertisements of the funds you will see them displaying four or five stars as a sign of a high ranking, a sign of being above average, from the service. These stars as a form of ratings mean nothing! In fact, almost 75 percent of the funds Morningstar follows get such four- and five-star rankings while only 25 percent receive the lower one- or two-star rankings.

The plot thickens. Wharton professor Martin Blume recently revealed that these four- and five-star rankings can be given to funds that have been in business for only three years. This is far too short a time to have confidence in how a fund will perform. The window is just too tight. Given a good three-year lucky upswing in the market, a new fund will look great, but have no experience in declining markets (or track record to pull down the hot three years' performance), as have the older funds, which are not as apt to get the high star ratings.

A recent chart in *Investor's Business Daily*, "Leading Funds over the Last Year," illustrates this point. The yearly results are of eight funds in 1994, a year the stock market was up 1.3 percent. Of the supposed top funds, five of the eight lost money that year!

For 1995 we have another fascinating set of cold, hard facts; the S&P 500 was up 37.6 percent. Only one of the eight mutual funds beat the market. Then along comes 1997, posting a 35.1 percent gain, yet only two of the funds did better. Perhaps there's more, or should I say less, to mutual fund performance than you thought or were told/sold.

Mark Hulbert's *Financial Digest* has been tracking the Morningstar rankings since 1991 and flatly states that the "top ranked funds have lagged the stock market by an average of 3 percent per year!"

Forbes magazine and *Value Line* also rank funds, and Hulbert's number crunching arrives at the same conclusion; these rankings have no ability to spot the best funds in the next time period. The bottom line is that the well-ranked funds underperformed the market in the future, in some cases by almost 5 percent a year.

Knowing that even the pros cannot pick the hot funds for the coming year leads us to ask, "Is it possible to time the funds?" If so, in theory, we could miss the big slides that hurt the funds' performance and we could sidestep bear markets.

The answer is a clear-cut: "Yes, you can beat the funds with a simple mechanical rule or two. It is possible to be out of the markets when the big crashes come."

Sure, it will take a little work to time the funds you are holding. It may take 15 minutes a week at the most, and many weeks there will be nothing to do.

As always, I'll first prove my point, then give you the formula you need to pull this all off.

Our first step will be to buy a mutual fund. Which one? It may not matter too much, based on the evidence I've just presented. The old reliable funds would include Kaufman, Oppenheimer Quest A, AIM Funds Aggressive Growth, Fidelity Low Priced, Fidelity Contrafund, Fidelity Inv., Destiny 1 or 2. Most brokerage firms have funds that have decent performances as well. What you are looking for is a growth fund that you can get in and out of for no fee (called a load) or a very small fee. Charles Schwab, Dean Witter, and Merrill Lynch all have funds you can throw your money at, and we know rankings, ratings, and the like don't mean much about future performance. Indeed, the only way we can buy the best-performing fund of the next time period is . . . to get lucky!

Several funds have "families of funds" that allow you to switch from their growth fund to a less aggressive fund or even a cash equivalent fund. Fidelity is perhaps the best example of this.

After you put your money down, one of two things will happen: The price or asset value will go up, or it will go down! The ups we don't worry about. We know stock prices, on average, move higher to the tune of about 9 percent a year.

The downs are what we have to worry about. In the long run a carefully selected growth-oriented mutual fund will make money for us. The problem is that in the long run—out there someplace—is a bear market just waiting to happen that will lop off 20 percent or more of the fund's value, seemingly stealing one-fifth of your money.

Our object, our desire, is to beat the funds by having a safety valve or off ramp to get us out before such an onslaught of selling tramples the growth our investments have made.

As you can tell, I'm a pretty down-to-earth guy. I don't act on whims and fancy rumors. I want, need, things documented as fact to stir me to the point of shelling out my hard-earned dollars. So should you.

$10,000 TO $8,000,000 TRADING FUNDS

The leading advocate of mutual fund timing and switching is a fellow named Richard Fabian. Dick has been a fund trader for more than a quarter of a century. In that time period he has clearly proven the advantages of timing funds, that it can be done. In real time, his advisory service and telephone hot line have beaten the funds. The service can be reached at 800-950-8765.

Nelson Freeburg, editor of *Formula Research* (901-767-1956), did an exhaustive study of the Fabian Formula in 1994 and concluded the "system has outperformed the stock market going back to 1929, the results were consistent across a broad range of parameters . . . the method has been put to test in the real world."

Freeburg goes on to point out that a strict buy and hold of stocks from 1929 forward shows an annual compound gain of 9.2 percent. Had you plunked down $10,000 way back then you'd have had $2.94 million by the end of 1993.

Using the Fabian Formula to time the market, your $10,000 would have grown to $8.10 million!

Do I have your attention?

Good, let me lay this on you: Of the 10 biggest one-day market declines since 1929 the Fabian Formula was on the sideline 80 percent of the time.

Is our risk limited when we use market timing? Yes, it is. In fact, the formula, according Freeburg carries almost 40 percent less statistical risk than the buy-and-hold approach. This is pretty obvious. If the method works it should bypass the big declines. Now here's the interesting point. The signals are just a little over 50 percent accurate, but the average gain has been about six times the average loss. Winners last 10 times longer than losers.

By now you should be clamoring at the bit for the rules, so here they are:

I Buy when the fund closes for the week above a 39-week moving average of the fund's weekly closes, and either the Dow Jones Industrials or Utilities have also closed above their 39-week average.

I Sell, to exit the long position, when the fund's weekly closing price is below the 39-week average, and either the Dow Industrials or Utilities have also closed below their 39-week average.

That's all there is to it. No other rules, as tested by Freeburg, though Fabian may have added a few twists in recent years.

You can use the Fabian Formula as given here or an improved variation Freeburg devised. His formula takes that $10,000 from 1929 to $11.7 million and with lower statistical risk than the original Fabian model.

The best example of this risk-reducing approach is in the time period from 1929 to 1939. Stocks, as measured by the averages, lost 2.1 percent a year, while the model you are about to learn showed a profit of 5.3 percent a year. Measuring risk by standard deviation, the formula was 31 percent less risky than the market itself.

Now to the rules:

I Buy when the Dow 30 index closes 2 percent above the lowest point of the market decline, and the Dow Transports are 4 percent above the lowest point of the market decline, and the Dow Utilities are 8 percent above the lowest point of the decline.

I Sell, move to cash, and liquidate the fund when the Dow is 2 percent below the highest high of the up move at *the same time* Transports are 4 percent below and the Utilities 8 percent below.

That's all there is to it. At any given time you can see if we are in an up-trend, then look for the signal of a 2 percent decline, 4 percent Transports dip, and 8 percent Utility dip. When all three averages have been bit by such trend changes it's time to leave the party.

An important consideration—Since very many market slides hit stocks the worst on Fridays and Mondays, I encourage you to create your own "week ending" data. By that I mean use the close of the averages on Thursday for your signals. If a signal comes on a Thursday close, exit the fund you are in and move to cash Friday morning. If no signal is given on a Thursday, but is on Friday, exit first thing Monday morning.

In fact, once you start running the numbers you will know, or can readily see, what type of closes will trigger a buy or sell and you can take action shortly before the close of business on Friday. Yes, I realize this takes a little more work on your part. But keep in mind that the vast majority of the time, week after week, prices will be trending and there will be no work to be done. Your work or close monitoring will take place only at times when a trend reversal is close at hand and it will pay to be alert, on your toes.

A wrap up on the ratios—The best ratio returns are:

Lowest price-to-sales	13.9%
Lowest price-to-book	17.1%
Lowest price to 1-year forward earnings	19.3%

12

MONEY MANAGEMENT: THE KEYS TO THE KINGDOM

I have made this letter longer than usual, because I lack the time to make it short.

—Blaise Pascal

The creation of a speculator's wealth comes from how he manages his money, not some magical, mysterious system or alchemist's secret. Successful investing makes money; successful investing with proper money management can create immense wealth.

Here it is, the most important chapter in this book, the most important chapter in my life, the most valuable thoughts I can transfer from me to you. I have nothing of more value that I could possibly give you than what you are about to learn. This is not an overstatement.

It is the formula I have used to take small amounts of money like $2,000 to over $100,000, and $100,000 to $1,000,000. Those were not hypothetical victories. We are not talking Monday morning quarterbacking here; we are talking real time, real money, real profits—profits you can spend, profits you can buy all the luxuries of life with.

Until you use a money management approach you will be a two-bit speculator, making some money here, losing some there, but never making a big score. The brass ring of commodity trading will always be out of your grasp as you sashay from one trade to another, picking up dollars but not amassing wealth.

The truly shocking thing about money management is how few people want to learn about it or to know the correct formulas. Invariably, when I am at a dinner or cocktail party the conversation turns to the markets. People want hot tips, or to know how I've been able to make a living without working. They want my secret. As if there is one!

The public or noneducated speculator thinks there is magic to trading, that somewhere, someplace, someone has a magic decoder ring that correctly signals market action.

Nothing could be further from the truth. Money is made in this business by getting an advantage in the game, working that advantage on a consistent basis, and coupling this with a consistent approach to how much of your bankroll you have behind each trade.

MOST TRADERS USE A HIT-OR-MISS APPROACH

The problem most investors have is that if we are confident enough to risk large sums of money, at least large for us, we are also confident enough to think we can figure out the future. That translates into two problem areas.

First, we think we can select the winning trades from the losers in our system or approach. Worse, though, is when, believing we are smart enough to do that, we then trade an unequal number of contracts or shares on our various trades.

Just as we must consistently follow our battle plan to succeed, we must also be consistent in the amount of money we martial behind each trade. The instant you get the fancy notion you can "for sure" pick the big winners and back those trades with larger positions than you have been trading, trouble will find you.

Granted, every now and then you will hit it right and score big, but eventually you will have a loss when you have on that large position. The loss is bad enough, but since you have overstepped good money management, you will then become emotional and probably hold onto the trade too long in hopes of recouping the big hit. Thus things don't get better, they get worse!

Let me turn to our well-worn Las Vegas casino analogy one more time. Casinos all over the world limit their losses by having a maximum amount the player can bet on any one decision in every game. They, like a good investor should, limit their losses. Can you imagine a pit boss suddenly allowing a high roller to bet more than the house limit because the boss feels the customer is going to lose on the next roll? Of course not; the pit boss would be fired on the spot for breaking a cardinal rule of money management, betting too much.

Trading too much, betting too much will cost you far more than bad market calls. Remember we control risk by limiting exposure to our bank roll.

APPROACHES TO MONEY MANAGEMENT: ONE IS RIGHT FOR YOU

There are various ways to go about this problem, many formulas to follow. But all the superior systems to manage your investment dollars have a common tenet: You will increase the number of units, contracts, or shares as you make money and decrease as you lose money. That is the essence of the sweet science of the correct marshalling of your funds. This basic truth can be worked on several ways.

I'm going to show you the major ones in hopes you find the shoe that fits you. No discussion on the subject could be complete if the name Ralph Vince is not brought up. In 1986 I ran across a money management formula for playing blackjack originally developed in a 1956 paper, "A New Interpretation of Information Data," regarding flow of information, now called the "Kelly formula" by commodity traders.

What I know about math you could add up with your thumb and first finger, but I know math works, so I began trading commodities using the Kelly formula. Here it is with F representing the amount of your account you will back every trade with:

$$\frac{F = (R + 1) \times P - 1}{R}$$

where P = Percentage accuracy of the system winning
  R = Ratio of winning trade to losing trade

Let's look at an example using a system that is 65 percent accurate with wins 1.3 times the size of losses. The math is done as follows using P as .65 and R as 1.3:

$$\frac{(1.3 + 1) \times .65 - 1}{1.3} = F$$

$$\frac{2.3 \times .65 = 1.495 - 1 = 0.495}{1.3} = \frac{38\% \text{ of account}}{\text{used to trade}}$$

In this example you would use 38 percent of your money behind every trade. If you had a $100,000 account you would use $38,000 and divide that by margin to arrive at the number of contracts. If margin was $2,000 you would be trading 19 contracts.

THE GOOD, THE BAD, AND THE UGLY OF MONEY MANAGEMENT

What this formula did for my trading results was phenomenal. In a very short time I became a real-life legend as very small amounts of money sky-rocketed. Using the percent of the money in the account based on the Kelly formula, divided by margin, was my approach. It was so good that I was actually kicked out of one trading contest because the promoter believed the results could not be accomplished without cheating! To this day, people on the Internet claim I used two accounts, one for winning trades and one for losers! They seem to forget, or not know, that in addition to such a practice being highly illegal, all trades must have an account number on them before the trade is entered, so how could the broker, or myself, know which trade should have the winning account number on it?

But what would you expect when no one, to my knowledge, had turned in that type of performance ever before in the history of trading? To make matters worse, I did it more than once. If it wasn't a fluke or luck. The losers lament is that it must have been done by pinching some numbers or trades along the way.

What I was doing was revolutionary. And, like with any good revolution, some blood flowed in the streets. The blood of disbelief was that first the National Futures Association and the Commodity Futures Trading Commission commandeered all my account records, looking for fraud!

The CFTC went through the brokerage firm's records with a fine-toothed comb, then took all my records and kept them for over a year before giving them back. About a year after getting them back, guess what, they wanted them back again. Success kills.

All this was due to market performance that was unheard-of. One of the accounts I managed went from $60,000 to some $500,000 in about 18 months using this new form of money management. Then the client sued me, her lawyer, saying she should have made $54,000,000 instead of half a million. Now my believers were willing to put me on a pedestal, if they could collect some money. The revolution was more than anyone could handle.

What a story, huh?

But there are two edges to this money management sword.

My extraordinary performance attracted lots of money for me to manage. Lots of money, and then it began to happen . . . the other side of the sword flashed in the sun. Amidst trying to now be a business manager (i.e., running a money management firm), with precious few skills at doing something I'm no good at anyway, my market system or approach hit the skids, encountering a cold streak that saw equally spectacular erosions of equity. While I had been making money hand over fist, I was now losing money hand over fist.

Brokers and clients screamed. Most took the off-ramps—they simply could not handle this type of volatility in their account balances. My own account, which had started the first of the year at $10,000 (yes, that is $10,000) and reached $2,100,000 (yes, that's $2.1 million) got hit along with everyone else's. It too was caught in the whirlpool, spiraling down to a meager $700,000.

About then everyone jumped ship, except me. Hey, I'm a commodity trader; I like roller coasters. Is there another form of life? Not that I knew, so I stayed on trading the account back to $1,100,000 by the end of 1987.

What a year!

Watching all this over my shoulder every day was Ralph Vince, while we were working together on systems and money management. Long before I could see it, he saw it, saw there was a fatal flaw in the Kelly formula. I was too dumb. I kept trading it while Ralph, being the math genius he is, began intense research into money management, the culmination of which are three great books. His first was *The Mathematics of Money Management*, followed by *Portfolio Management Formulas*, and my favorite, *The New Money Management*, all published by John Wiley & Sons, Inc. These are must-reads for any serious trader or money manager.

Ralph noticed the error of Kelly, that it was originally formulated to assist in implementing the flow of electricity, then used for blackjack. The rub comes from the simple fact that blackjack is not commodity or stock trading. In blackjack your potential loss on each wager is limited to the chips you put up, while your potential gain will always be the same in relation to the chips bet.

We speculators don't have such an easy life. The size of our wins and losses bounces all over the place. Sometimes we get big winners, sometimes minuscule ones. Our losses reflect the same pattern; they are random in size.

Now the reality is that this system may not hold up in the future exactly like this. You will probably not want to trade up to 5,000 bonds, which this test allowed. In that case one tick, the smallest price change bonds can have, would cost you $162,500 if that one tick is against you. I've been there . . . that's real pressure. Let me add, it is not unusual for bonds to open 8 to 10 ticks against you. Every morning, that's $1,625,000! So, don't get carried away with the profits. Focus on the impact of the results money management can produce.

As soon as Ralph realized this, he could explain the wild gyrations in my equity swings, that they came about because we were using the wrong formula. This may seem pretty basic as we have a new century, but back then we were in the midst of a revolution in money management and this stuff was not easy to see. We were tracking and trading where, to the best of my knowledge, no one had gone before. What we saw were some phenomenal trading results, so we did not want to wander too far from whatever it was we were doing.

Ralph came up with an idea he calls Optimal F. It's similar to Kelly, but unlike Kelly it can adapt to trading markets and gives you a fixed percent of your account balance to bankroll all your trades.

LOOKING IN NEW DIRECTIONS: DRAWDOWN AS AN ASSET

My trading stumbled along with spectacular up and down swings, while we continued looking for an improvement, something, anything that would tame the beast. From this search came the basic idea that we needed a formula that would tell us how many contracts or shares to take on the next trade.

One such thought was to divide our account balance by margin plus the largest drawdown the system had seen in the past. This sure makes a lot of sense. You are certain to get hit by a similar, if not larger, drawdown in the future, so you had better have enough money for that plus margin. As a matter of fact, it struck me that one would need an amount equal to margin plus drawdown times 1.5 just to be on the safe side.

Thus if margin was $3,000 and the system's largest drawdown in the past had been $5,000, you would need $10,500 to trade one contract [$3,000 + ($5,000 × 1.5)]. This is not a bad formula, but it does have some problems.

I'm not going to be showing a variety of money management schemes applied to the same system. The system is one of the best I have, so the results will look a little too good. What you should focus on is the differences in performance that are the product of the different approaches to managing your money. The system trades bonds, which have a $3,000 margin. The first printout reflects the complete results of the system from January 1990 through mid-July 1998. (See Figure 12.1.)

Now we'll take this same system and apply a variety of money management strategies so you can see which one might best work for you. To arrive at the various inputs I ran the system for just the first seven years, then traded forward with money management for the remaining time period so the drawdown, percent accuracy, risk/reward ratios, and the like were developed on sample data and run on out-of-sample data. I allowed the system to trade up to 5,000 bonds, which is a heck of a lot.

RYAN JONES AND FIXED RATIO TRADING

Another friend, Ryan Jones, went at trying to solve money management like a man possessed. He initially was a student at one of my seminars, and I later went to his on my favorite subject, money management. Ryan has thought about the problem a great deal and spent thousands of dollars and research formulating is solution called Fixed Fractional Trading.

Like Ralph Vince and me, Ryan wanted to avoid the blowup phenomena inherent in the Kelly formula. His solution is to wander away from a fixed ratio approach of trading X contracts for every Y dollars in your account.

His reasoning is based largely on his dislike for increasing the number of contracts too rapidly. Consider an account with $100,000 that will trade one contract for every $10,000 in the account, meaning it will start trading 10 contracts or units. Let's assume the average profit per trade is $250, meaning we will make $2,500 (10 contracts times $250) and need five trades to increase to trading 11 contracts. All goes well and we keep making money until we are up $50,000 with a net balance of $150,000, meaning we are now trading 15 contracts, which nets us $3,750 per win; thus we increase an additional contract after only three trades. At $200,000 of profits we make $5,000 per trade, thus needing only two winners to step up another contract.

Ryan's approach is to require a fixed ratio of money to be made to bump up one contract. If it takes $5,000 in profits to jump from one to two contracts, it will take $50,000 in profits on a $100,000 account to go

System Number: 387   Description: bonds 7/98 no bail
System Rules:
Market: Test Period: 1/1/90 to 7/16/98

Summary

Trades	310	Begin Balance	$ 30,000
PL Ratio	1.4	Ending Balance	$18,107,546
Drawdown TT	($3,988)	Equity Peak	$18,107,546
Drawdown PV	−61.3%	Return	60258.5%

Profitable Trades ——————— Losing Trades

Wins	230	Losses	80
Win Pct	74.2%	Loss Pct	25.8%
Win Avg	$1,350.68	Loss Avg	$985.55
Largest Win	$10,137.50	Largest Loss	($1,956.25)
Most Consec Wins	31	Most Consec Losses	6
Avg Consec Wins	4.11	Avg Consec Losses	1.45

Number of trades to reach the maximum units traded	310
Number of days to reach the maximum units traded	0

Base Unit Calculation Rules

BASE Units = account balance/(draw down #2)
If Account Balance Increases by: units last trade
INCREASE units on the next trade by: 1
If Account Balance Decreases by: units last trade
DECREASE units on the next trade by: 1

Figure 12.1 Varied Results Based on Risk Percent of Account
Source: Genesis Financial Data.

from 10 to 11 units. The fixed ratio is that if it took 15 trades, on average, to go from one to two contracts it will always take 15 trades, on average, to bump up to that next level, unlike Ralph's fixed ratio that requires fewer trades to go to higher levels.

Ryan accomplishes this by using a variable input (one you can alter to suit your personality) as a ratio to drawdown. He seems to prefer using the largest drawdown divided by 2. We will now look at the same trading system for the bond market with the Ryan Jones formula (see Figure 12.2).

As you can see, this approach also creates wealth in that in brings about an exponential growth of your account. However, to achieve the same growth as with the other formulas you need to pony up a larger percent of your bankroll on each bet. This can result in a wipeout scenario as well, as you will see in a minute, unless, you use a very low percent of your money, which in return guarantees a less rapid growth in your account.

System Report   *9/11/98   11:54:44 AM*

System Number: 387   Description: bonds 7/98 no bail
System Rules:
Market: Test Period: 1/1/90 to 7/16/98

Summary

Trades	310	Begin Balance	$ 20,000
PL Ratio	1.4	Ending Balance	$251,813
Drawdown TT	($3,988)	Equity Peak	$251,813
Drawdown PV	−18.3%	Return	1159.1%

Profitable Trades ——————— **Losing Trades**

Wins	230	Losses	80
Win Pct	74.2%	Loss Pct	25.8%
Win Avg	$1,350.68	Loss Avg	$985.55
Largest Win	$10,137.50	Largest Loss	($1,956.25)
Most Consec Wins	31	Most Consec Losses	6
Avg Consec Wins	4.11	Avg Consec Losses	1.45

Number of trades to reach the maximum units traded	43
Number of days to reach the maximum units traded	370

Base Unit Calculation Rules

ONE CONTRACT
ONLY

Figure 12.2 Bond Trading System without Money Management
Source: Genesis Financial Data.

AND NOW MY SOLUTION TO THE PROBLEM

In talks with Ralph and Ryan I was made aware that what was causing the wild gyrations was not the percent accuracy of the system, nor was it the win-loss ratio or drawdown. The hitch and glitch came from the largest losing trade. Let me explain—this is a very important concept.

In system development it is easy to fool ourselves by creating a system that is 90 percent accurate, making scads of money, but will eventually kill us. That doesn't sound possible, does it? Well it is, and here's how. Our 90 percent system makes $1,000 on each winning trade and has nine winners in a row, leaving us ahead by a cool 9 G's. Then comes a losing trade of $2,000, netting us $7,000, not bad. We get nine more winners and are sitting pretty with $16,000 of profits when we get another loss, but this one is a big one, a loss of $10,000, the largest allowed by the system, setting us back on our fannies with only $6,000 in our pockets.

But, since we had been playing the game by increasing after making money, we had two contracts on and thus lost $20,000. We were actually in the hole $4,000 despite 90 percent accuracy! I told you this money management stuff was important.

What ate us alive was that large losing trade. That's the devil we need to protect against, and incorporate into our money management scheme.

The way I do this is first determine how much of my money I want to risk on any one trade. I'm a risk seeker so, for sake of argument and illustration, let's say I'm willing to risk 40 percent of my account balance on one trade.

If my balance is $100,000, that means I've got $40,000 and since I know the most I can lose is, say, $5,000, I divide $5,000 into $40,000 and discover I can trade eight contracts. The problem is if I get two large losers in a row I'm down 80 percent, so we know 40 percent is too much risk. Way too much.

Generally speaking you will want to take 6 percent to 12 percent of your account balance, divide that by the largest dollar loss you will allow, or loss you are willing to take, to arrive at the number of shares you will trade. A very risk-oriented trader might trade close to 20 percent of his/her account on one trade, but keep in mind, three max losers in a row and you have lost 60 percent of your money.

I'm next showing the same system we've been using in this chapter with various risk percentages divided by the largest loss in this system, which is locked in by a $1,600 stop loss. As you can see, the more you risk the more you make, and the larger your drawdowns will become (see Figure 12.3).

Next, I've graphed out the increase in the account equity with the in-

System Report   *9/11/98   3:00:45 PM*

System Number: 387   Description: bonds 7/98 no bail
System Rules:
Market: Test Period: 1/1/90 to 7/16/98

┌─ Summary ──┐

Trades	310	Begin Balance	$ 30,000
PL Ratio	1.4	Ending Balance	$582,930,624
Drawdown TT	($3,988)	Equity Peak	$582,930,624
Drawdown PV	−29.7%	Return	1943002.1%

┌─ Profitable Trades ─────────── Losing Trades ──────────┐

Wins	230	Losses	80
Win Pct	74.2%	Loss Pct	25.8%
Win Avg	$1,350.68	Loss Avg	$985.55
Largest Win	$10,137.50	Largest Loss	($1,956.25)
Most Consec Wins	31	Most Consec Losses	6
Avg Consec Wins	4.11	Avg Consec Losses	1.45

Number of trades to reach the maximum units traded	223
Number of days to reach the maximum units traded	2152

Base Unit Calculation Rules

BASE UNITS = account balance*.15/largest loss

Figure 12.3   Varied Results Based on Risk Percent of Account
Source: Genesis Financial Data.

crease in drawdown directly below it. As you can see, there is a point where the amount you make rises faster than the drawdown, then as the risk percent increases, drawdown increases faster than the increase in profits in your account. This usually takes place between 14 percent and 21 percent. In most systems, any risk percent value greater than 25 percent will make more money but at a sharp increase in the drawdown. (See Figure 12.4.)

*So there it is, my money management formula: (Account balance ×
Risk percent)/Largest loss = Contracts or shares to trade.*

There are probably better and more sophisticated approaches, but for

System

Begin Balance $0.00

Ending Balance	Peak/Valley Drawdown	Risk Pct	Max Units	Restart Pct	Min Profit	Trading Style	Recover Losses	Margin
$845,429,594	−66.9%	40%	5000	100%	$0.00	All trades	No	$3,000.00
844,881,388	−77.1	50	5000	100	$0.00	All trades	No	$3,000.00
842,428,863	−72.2	45	5000	100	$0.00	All trades	No	$3,000.00
835,954,544	−61.5	35	5000	100	$0.00	All trades	No	$3,000.00
802,829,038	−54.4	30	5000	100	$0.00	All trades	No	$3,000.00
759,721,131	−46.6	25	5000	100	$0.00	All trades	No	$3,000.00
686,869,688	−38.2	20	5000	100	$0.00	All trades	No	$3,000.00
560,344,731	−28.4	15	5000	100	$0.00	All trades	No	$3,000.00
18,606	−7.0	10	5000	100	$0.00	All trades	No	$3,000.00

Figure 12.4   Top Nine Optimization Results
Source: Genesis Financial Data.

us run-of-the mill investors, not blessed with a deep understanding of math, this is the best I know of. The beauty of it is that you can tailor it to your risk/reward personality. If you are Tommy Timid, use 5 percent of your bank. Should you think you are Norm Normal, use 10 percent to 12 percent. If you are Leveraged Larry, use from 15 percent to 18 percent. And if you are Swashbuckling Sam or Dangerous Dan, use in excess of 20 percent of your account . . . and go to church regularly.

I have made millions of dollars with this approach. What more can I tell you? You have just been handed the keys to the kingdom of speculative wealth.

All equity runs and money management printouts in this chapter are from Ultimanager, a remarkable piece of software that allows you to test a wide variety of money management and trade selection techniques for any system. The software will teach you about your system or approach. Here are some examples: It will tell you if you should add more contracts after X number of winning or losing trades, inform you to add or subtract contracts following a big winning or losing trade, tell you what to do if you have a 70 percent accurate system that's running 30 percent on the last X number of trades, and on and on. If this software can't improve your system's performance, it can't be done. Developed by Mark Thorn, it can be purchased from Genesis Data at 800-808-3282 and can do full portfolio analysis.

13

FINAL THOUGHTS: NONRANDOM THOUGHTS ON A RANDOM MARKET

You only get out of life what you put into it.
—R. S. Williams—my father

The precise up and down moves of the next 2 to 20 years are impossible to predict. Nonetheless, I would like to go out on a limb in this chapter to make overall comments on what I think will be of value to short-term as well as long-term investors.

The recorded history of the past 200 years of stock market activity makes one statement: Despite up and down moves in the market, it is on a continual path upward, ever upward. Never forget that fact of stock market life. You can count on it having substantial corrections, or dips, along the way. Those are buying opportunities. Generally speaking, most bear markets decline by about 20 percent. Sometimes we will be fortunate enough to step in and buy right at the end of the declines.

At other times, however, there simply is no market decline. The market may have gone sideways for a while and then suddenly takes off with fury to the upside. Prices did not decline prior to blastoff. They simply muddled around. So, in this case our 20 percent decline rule is of no help. Perhaps even an extremely negative reading of investment advisers is not going to be present. What will most likely tip the prospect of a coming bull market will be the cyclical time factors mentioned earlier. I think we need to pay a great deal of attention to these time zones. I have noticed, concerning the four-year phenomenon, that if the bottom four years ago occurred in May it most likely will occur close to May this year. There's one pointer for you.

There is another pattern I have noticed in individual stocks that lead the way off of major market bottoms. The pattern is simply one of price, one I would like to show you at this time. As we approach these major buying opportunities you'll see stocks making step-down moves in the averages. By this I mean that each declines to a value, rallies, then declines to a lower value. Ultimately, the low of the bear market is made and prices rally off this point.

Here's the secret of selecting which stocks to buy at the start of a buy market. Stocks that do not go to a new market low while the averages go a low are most likely the ones to be the leaders on the upside. There's good logic to this idea. After all, the stock is in real strong hands. It resisted a major decline in the overall market, which took prices to the lows. Its reluctance to decline tells us that people who own the stock are unwilling to dump it even during the heat of the passion of negative influences that have impacted the rest of the stock market.

Figure 13.1 shows what this pattern looks like. If the same time mar-

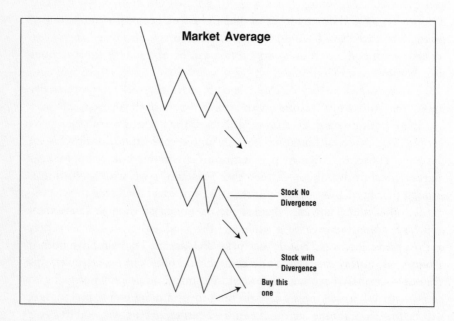

Figure 13.1   Stair Step Pattern

ket averages have gone to a new low our stock has had a rally but on the next leg down is able to hold above the prior low, we can say the stock is comparatively stronger than the Dow Jones or other market averages. Hence the stock, on a comparative basis (perhaps not relative basis), has been outperforming the majority of other stocks. This is the one we want to buy, not one that is now making the lows with the averages. This divergence tells us the stock is in good hands. Accordingly, I would expect it to rally more on the upside than other stocks.

The only caveat here is that you don't want to buy stocks that are countercyclical to the market averages.

INITIAL PUBLIC OFFERINGS

Many investors have seen the tremendous price increases of stocks from an initial public offering (IPO). There are many instances where the stocks doubled or tripled in a very short time. However, it really all gets down to what the market itself has been doing. Sometimes IPOs perform well, but when times are not good IPOs don't do so well. In 2000 and 2001 they underperformed the entire stock market by a dramatic amount.

While the S&P 500 was down 14 percent, the new issue index was down a staggering 79 percent. That's even worse than the Nasdaq, which was off 60 percent. There are no free lunches on Wall Street! IPO investing can be positive and negative. Why? First of all, these are relatively new companies that have just entered the big boys' arena. Some of the stocks and companies will perform well in the future, but others are based on hype and dreams. There are more dreams and hype late in a bull market than in the beginning of a bull market. If we think we're at the beginning of a bull market, we might want to take some select positions in IPOs, but late in the game there's no way I want to touch these types of stocks.

There is very little history on these IPOs. Some of them have been in existence for only three years, and had a blockbuster three-year report. But they may also have maximized their market position, or are "hip stocks," a trend that will soon quickly fade, leaving investors holding the bag. These stocks are "concept stocks," and concepts being figments of people's imaginations, can change quickly.

LOOKING INTO MY CRYSTAL BALL

Nobody on Wall Street has a very clear crystal ball. It's hazy for all of us. If we stop and think we can come up with some pretty good ideas of what most likely will happen in the economy over the next few years. Here are some thoughts I'd like to share with you about what I think is going on in the American economic system. First of all, the most underlying thing I see in economy is we continue to be a consumer-driven economy. We have so many people, and they have so much money, that there is simply nothing that can permanently stop the overall progress of mankind and our economic system. The business of business is now people—serving them, taking care of them, entertaining them. At all levels there are huge opportunities. These people companies will be as successful and as spectacular as any high-tech company.

While there will continue to be a great deal of focus on high-tech, scientific dream teams, who possess the answer to all medical woes and creature comforts, I don't think these are nearly as safe bets as companies that are selling things used virtually every single day.

One area that I find of particular interest is that of energy.

I've watched over the years and heard the cry of "energy crisis." Going back in history I see this first occurred around 1920, then again in the 1940s, in the 1950s, and during Jimmy Carter's presidential time, when we reached perhaps the peak of the energy crisis. The Cassandras, at that time were telling us we did not have enough energy to last until the end of the century. Well, here we are in 2001 and we still a plenty of energy. Yes, it does cost more now than it did, but what doesn't? On a relative basis gasoline is still extremely cheap. The cost of one gallon of Nyquill sells for about $98. Compare that to the cost of one gallon of gasoline.

Or, go by a gallon of Evian water, when I last checked that was selling for about six dollars a gallon. To produce that Evian water one didn't have to drill down 6,000 to 10,000 feet below the crust of the surface of the earth, suck it back up, then transport it to a refinery where the process of incredible pressures and heats begins. The folks at Evian didn't have to have a special trucking and piping system to get the finished product to specific stores where their product could be purchased.

All they had to do was get water out of a spring, put it in bottles, and ship to the stores all over the world . . . for six dollars a gallon. Now, I do not like high gasoline prices better than the next, but gasoline is cheap compared to most commodities.

I suspect, however, we're going to see continuing increases in energy prices, because there are fewer places open for exploration. Unless there is some new wisdom that suddenly prevails or wakes up the American public to the trade-offs between the importance of mankind versus natural resources (animals and tundra), we're going to be gridlocked in a battle of people wanting to explore for more energy and those not wanting the energy to be explored for. Hydrogen fuel cells are the answer and certainly the wave—and save—of our future. The strongest companies in this new technology are great growth stocks.

This is obviously a perfect investment scenario. It doesn't take a crystal ball to predict energy prices are going to go up. Trade accordingly. I suspect that energy companies will be doing better in the future, and they haven't done so poorly in the past.

The big focus, at this time, is on medical costs, HMOs and the like. One thing we can say for sure about the cost of health is that it has not gone down; it has only gone up. This will continue to happen. As an investor I think one of the poorest investments most people make is that of buying insurance, whether life insurance or health insurance. Here's a comment certain to strike people as being unsound.

Let me tell you why I think it is a bad investment; if you're responsible for your health, as opposed to simply handing that problem, and the bills, over to an insurance company, you take much better care of yourself. Insurance companies are not in business to be good guys, they are in business to make money. If you have health insurance you pay something called a premium. If your health claims paid by the insurance company exceed your premiums, the insurance company loses money. Since it is not in business to lose money, that means, on average, if you can self-insure yourself you'll be better off than paying a premium to an insurance company.

I realized there are extenuating circumstances to this. Some of us are basically healthier than others. Some are more health challenged than others. Some of us take better care of ourselves than others. You have to make that decision on your own. But whenever it comes to insurance I would rather take that money and invest it, earning, say, 20 percent a year, rather than losing that amount of money to an insurance company or health provider. It's just like leasing a car. The leasing companies make 18 percent per year on the car you lease. That's a great rate of return, better than many mutual funds do in the stock market, and better than many realtors do with their own investments.

You want to have your money earning that 18 percent a year as opposed to paying that 18 percent a year to banks, leasing companies, and the like.

Remember when I talked about the ideal fundamental setup for companies? I talked about the importance of companies having no or low debt. It's true in our lives as well. The more credit card debt, lease debt, even home debt you have, the less opportunity you have to build a portfolio or nest egg to invest with. Buying now, debt now, spending now, ultimately creates less, especially less for those retirement years when things really do matter.

A LOOK AT THE COMMODITY MARKETS

While Wall Street may have caught your fancy, you may also want to turn your attention to LaSalle Street. That's the street in Chicago where you'll find the Chicago Board of Trade—the futures markets where investors and traders speculate on real things. When you stop to think about it, nobody needs a share of Microsoft or a share of IBM. You can live the rest of your life without owning a stock.

But you can't live the rest of your life without cotton, copper, wheat, soybeans, soybean oil, silver, gold, and a wide variety of other commodities that are traded on these exchanges. Thus, we have better supply and demand figures in these markets than we do in the stock market. If you study the history of futures and commodities you'll see they have been primarily in large downtrends the past several years. At some point the situation will have to change. Farmers and ranchers can produce food for this nation and the world only so long without making much money. At some point the scales will tip. It may be because there's a drought or demand exceeds supply. For sure at some point this imbalance will have to change. When this does, there should be some wonderful bull markets in these natural resource commodities.

You may not have to purchase commodities directly to take advantage of this. You may want to follow companies that are commodity driven, such as, say, Starbucks in terms of coffee; ConAgra, a large commodity company; Archer Daniels; Hershey's; General Mills; and on the list goes.

One can usually determine when there'll be a shortage of a commodity in one of two ways. The first and simplest of these we will want to follow comes from data reported by the U.S. government each week. These weekly reports show how much buying and selling was being done by various members of the investment community. Each week we can find out if these commercial interests were buying or selling and in which commodity. When they get extreme in their position, that is, they are predominantly long, markets most often rally. By the same token, when they are heavily short markets most often decline.

Figure 13.2 of corn provides just one more example of this powerful relationship. At the beginning of 2000 the commercials were heavy short sellers in this marketplace, and that's why corn declined, in my opinion. In the middle of the year the commercials built up a large long position as they began buying this market in an aggressive fashion. Lo and behold, the

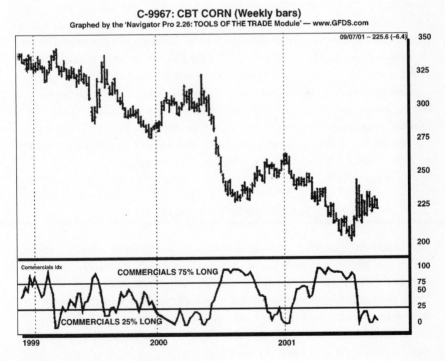

Figure 13.2   Corn versus Commercials

price of corn rallied until the start of 2001 when the commercials were back to the short side. As the year opened they were only 15 percent long in terms of the way I measure their activity. That means 85 percent of them were short at that time. So guess what. The price of corn declined until midyear when the grain markets shot to the upside in a brief flurry of bullish activity.

If we look at the same data in the gold market we can see what powerful influence these commercial people are. At the end of the first quarter of 2000 gold staged a strong rally, yet the commercial interests reflected a position of 92 percent short and 8 percent long. It's no wonder the price of gold then declined into June 2000 when the commercials were 58 percent long, setting up a rally that lasted until the commercials went short the market with an 86 percent net short position. They again reach a high buying level in November 2000, and of course gold prices rallied.

They became quite bullish, with a 71 percent reading in the winter of 2001, and gold started a real hot, quick, splashy rally to the upside, then moved sideways only to back and fill until May when the commercials were again 98 percent short this market. Only 2 percent of them were long! I remember this time so well. Subscribers of mine, and particular the gold bug camp, were screaming about how the price of gold was going to at long last begin the huge rally the gold bugs had been looking for all these years. That was possible; it could have happened.

But it would have been unlikely because the majority of the time when the commercials are excessively long prices rally. The majority of the time commercials are excessively short, as in this example, prices decline.

The ensuing down moving in gold came as no surprise to any of the people who have followed my work over the past 30 years.

TRANSPORTATION PROBLEM

The highly mobile society we now live in has produced some wonderful upcoming opportunities in the transportation industry. Because trains are essentially dying out (the sooner the better in my opinion), the airlines have had a wonderful opportunity to make money, yet many of them have not. Why should that be so? There are some specific reasons, such as in the San Francisco area, thanks to its fog, where bad weather wreaks havoc and creates delayed planes and angry passengers.

But, by and large, airlines have not been responsive to the needs of passengers, and have huge debt. Airlines such as Southwest are flying high and making money, and the prices of their stocks have been going up. The unresponsive airlines (I would point out United Air Lines as one) have suffered in the marketplace.

This we know for sure; there is a huge amount of money being spent in transportation every year. Airplanes have made this an increasingly shrinking, smaller world. Therefore, if you see a transportation company that is delivering the goods and the people on time and in a comfortable fashion there is a gargantuan market for them. They will be able to increase sales, which should increase the bottom-line earnings reports. That means they'll have lower price-to-sales ratios, higher P/E ratios, and higher dividend yield payments—exactly what we're looking for.

This entire area of transportation fascinates me because I don't think the world will slow down; people are going to travel more in the future than they ever have in the past. Whatever company allows that to happen in the easiest and most convenient fashion is going to find the gold at the end of the rainbow.

FINANCIAL SERVICES

The financial industry has gone from an old boys' network where deals were done on a napkin in bars to a high-tech, highly organized, and computerized business enterprise. I'm certain J. P. Morgan, Dean Witter, or any of the founders of Merrill Lynch would be both amazed and dismayed by the current status of these organizations.

If I'm right in my hunch that there will continue to be more money in the future, that there is no big crash or depression coming, then the future is one of many people having much money. Unfortunately, money does not create character. But then again, character will never be produced by money.

Some people will put their money under a mattress. Some will only seek savings accounts. Will that be the majority? I don't think so. I think the majority are going to turn to professionals to invest their money. There are only a handful of people, like you, my dear reader, who have the initiative, the driving intelligence, to enter this world of investments on their own. The bulk of people are lazy, complacent, and to their detriment, believe professionals can do a better job than they. Oh, these poor misguided souls!

But that's our problem. Our problem, rather an opportunity, is determining what these people will do with all their money. Many will turn their dollars over to the local banker or insurance salesperson, more will place their money with brokerage firms and mutual funds, and a very few will invest in commodity funds. The world is wide open for investment managers and people who are willing to take on the responsibility, and awesome task, of managing other people's money. This should be an opportunity we do not walk by. It means our focus can be on mutual funds and major brokerage firms. Their business can only grow. The big ones are the ones most likely to stay in business and continue to expand their business, so folks like Charles Schwab, Merrill Lynch, Bear Stearns, Goldman Sachs, and the like need to be followed. The bigger the firms, the bigger I believe their market shares will become. Accordingly, you should make note of this significant industry. It does not have the jazz and sex appeal of high tech, drugs, and medicine, but money is as much a part of life as getting sick. If you believe in going where the money is, or will be, this is the place.

Come to think of it, more people probably get sick over money than anything else!

ENTERTAINMENT INDUSTRY

Consumers are pretty predictable lot: They wake up in the morning, go to work, come home, and then look for something to do. Unfortunately, for the most part, their lives are full of drudgery. They don't have excitement and passion, and what they do it is becoming a humdrum existence, whether in the office or the factory. Most people's lives are not very thrilling. They need to escape, to get outside of this condition.

That's why entertainment will be such a huge market in the future. Even now, we see what to me is an appalling attention placed on movies and concerts. It's just my personal view, but I want to say, "Get a life." There's more to do and to watch than stupid movies and so many of them now are just that. Go to concerts for about $100 to hear the same thing you can hear on a $10 CD? I don't think so. But that's just me. I'm not of the masses. I'm not into crowd activity. These people need some rush and excitement in their lives, so they turn to movies and concerts, television, and the like to provide for them (as well as drugs). Notice the words "provide for them." These people are so used to being couch potatoes, to being entertained, they never consider doing something entertaining.

There is a smaller minority of people who like to camp, hike, travel, or exercise. These are the people who participate, people who are onstage in the great play of life. There are markets here that an investor should pay attention to. But that market is not nearly as big as the market that provides entertainment at home to basic couch potatoes.

Invest in Couch Potatoes

There are all sorts of things that might change in terms of the entertainment business. Consider this: Currently on television, we see many reruns of yesterday's movies. Movies are not cheap to produce. A good movie now costs $50 million. But consider the possibilities of having a really good movie done with major stars and showing it as a first-run feature, not in theaters but on television. How many homes could you sell a movie to starring Mel Gibson, Julia Roberts, and Tom Hanks if the price was $2 for the movie? I suspect it would be a snap to sell to at lease 25 million homes and recap your investment all in one night.

The couch potato crowd would love this; they don't even have to go out and rent the movie at the local Blockbuster. They simply get a first-run movie, never seen before, with major stars for two bucks. Fifty million homes in the first month nets $100 million—not bad. The beauty of television is it can deliver so much, to so many people, so cheaply. I suspect we're going to see a switch in television from the traditional news, game shows, and junk shows to making it more similar to traditional entertainment, filling the role that movies, stage, and concerts have had in our lives.

In any event, this is an industry we should pay close attention to. Certainly stocks like Disney, MGM, the cable television giants, and such need to be monitored by savvy investors.

OPPORTUNITY ABOUNDS—ALWAYS HAS, ALWAYS WILL

Seldom do markets go straight up as they did in 1998 and 1999. The coming years will most likely be a wild swinging affair presenting us with some wonderful bull markets that turn into declines, which give way to yet one more bull market. On and on it will go to the end of time. The best long-term bet is to the bull side. I do not know exactly how it will unfold; no one does. I hope you now know when the best times to invest are most likely to appear and what fundamentals are the most profitable for us to take action upon.

The future will bring us changes we cannot even think of at this point, whether in corporate profits or great cash flow, price-to-book, and price-to-sales ratios. There will be wars and destruction, bad times and good times. It is a speculator's task to weave in and out of these opportunities, to seek personal freedom (which is usually against the law) and prosper.

I wish you well. I wish you prosperity. The future is there. Grab it and prosper.

MORE FUEL TO THE FIRE

Finally, here's a most innovative chart from Tom McClellan that looks at money in circulation by the Fed (M3), divided by the rate of change of the Dow Jones Industrial Average.

Going back to 1962, you can easily see that when the rate of change is high, there is money in circulation and stocks have been a solid buy. His point, and it's a good one, is that value alone is not enough to create a bull market—money is what fuels the rallies.

Clearly, in April 2003 there is money—or fuel—for a bull market.

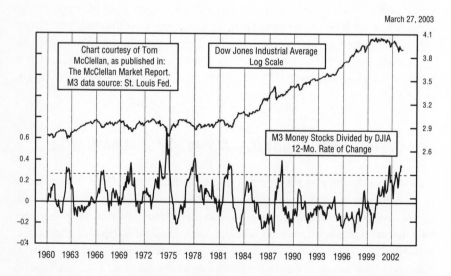

© 2003, McClellan Financial Publications, Inc. www.mcoscillator.com, (800) 872-3737.

INDEX